# The 7 Figures Plan

A simple system to achieve clarity in your finances:
take action now to secure the future you want

## Dan Woodruff

To 3 women who inspire me to be better in everything I do:

To my mum, Maureen:
I still miss our long, late-night discussions about the future,
putting the world to rights.

To my wife, Magali:
We build a wonderful life together every day.
When I imagined my life with my future partner, I thought of you.

To my daughter, Olivia:
I look forward to seeing you grow into the woman you will become.
I am already proud of you.

# CONTENTS

# Chapter 1 - Why you should read this book

## About the author

I want to tell you about a day that changed my life. At the time, Financial Planning meant nothing to me, but what happened that day influenced my philosophy on this subject.

It was a Saturday in April 1991 and I was 16 years old. I was watching the football FA Cup semi-final featuring Tottenham Hotspur v Arsenal. I am a Spurs fan and Arsenal is our closest rival, so it was a big day for me. It was also the first semi-final to be played at the national stadium at Wembley, so there was an extra edge to the match. It was a great day for Spurs fans, one which will live long in the memory – Paul Gascoigne scored an amazing goal, and my team won 3-1. I should have been delighted, but I wasn't.

During the game my mum came back from a doctor's appointment and told us that she had been diagnosed with Multiple Sclerosis. It was a terrible revelation. I remember her being unwell for months before that day, but she was experiencing intermittent symptoms. The lives of the whole family changed at that point. I did all I could at that moment; I held her hand and told her that everything would be alright. Of course, I didn't really believe it. My mum was a few days short of her 35th birthday.

Multiple Sclerosis is one of those difficult conditions which defy medical advances. Treatments are better now, but there weren't many viable options in those days. My mum's condition became progressively worse until eventually she became bed-bound. Her life really shrank in those years, but I admire her strength of will to carry on regardless. She died suddenly on my brother's 21st birthday at just 50 years old.

Why do I bring all this up? Not out of a desire to make you feel sorry for her or me. I am sure that you know many stories like this, and something similar (or worse) may have happened in your family. I tell you this story because this experience really shaped my vision over why and how I should practise Financial Planning.

I started my Financial Planning business a few years before my mum died. At the time, I was frustrated with my career with a large insurance company. I thought that I saw an opportunity to do things differently in the local market. I didn't realise it then, but my mum's death at an early age, and my reflections on the difficulties of her life, would come to shape how I saw the world and my business. In fact, the changes had already begun within me, but I hadn't yet realised them.

I think now that I can trace back my philosophy on Financial Planning and the world in general directly to those experiences. As a direct result of what I saw my mum go through I believe that we owe it to ourselves to live the best and fullest life we can – whatever that means to each of us. Life can be short and it can be brutal, and we really don't know what is around the corner. Therefore, we had better be prepared and we had better make the most of it while we are fit and able enough to enjoy it. Of course, I do not advocate living your life purely for now. You need to strike a balance between living while you are fit and able to, but you should also prepare for a secure future. This book will show you how you can achieve that.

## My professional background

So what qualifies me to lay all this out for you? Here's a short history of my professional career. I finished school with good grades and naturally went to university to study Law and Politics. My plan was to qualify as a solicitor and I saw my professional life mapped out before me. I went on to do the postgraduate vocational study that all English solicitors do. While looking for legal work I took a job in a major insurance company thinking I would bide out my time until I found a law job. I hated working there, but I did find that I was earning 3 times what I could have earned as a trainee solicitor, and had a shiny company car as well. The money made it difficult to go back to the law, and each year that went past led me to put aside that goal. Sometimes I regret not pursuing the legal career hard enough, but we all have to recognise that we take decisions based on the circumstances at the time. Actually, I now question whether I would have been happy in a traditional professional career.

After 2 years, I moved to another insurance company with a better fit for my values and found out that there was another world in financial advice. Previously, I had worked for a company which only promoted its own products. I was young and didn't really fully understand the nature of the financial world. I sometimes smile when I remember that I was trying to give financial advice to people double or triple my age, despite having little or no experience with money! The new company dealt with Independent Financial Advisers, who could recommend products to clients from any financial institution. I consulted with a panel of financial advisers and tried to get them to use this company's products. I learned a lot from this experience about the profession and also how financial advisers worked in those days. In those days most financial advice was transactional; they would focus on getting the next sale and it was all driven by commission. My best route to market was to find those advisers who needed technical help and to help them out. A lot of the time we did much of the work for them and it started to get a bit depressing. After 5 years there in 2003 I decided to set up my Financial Planning business, convinced I could do things in a better way. From the start I was tried to focus on comprehensive Financial Planning – the kind of subjects outlined in this book. However, it took a while to build up my skills and clients in this area, and my business approach has gone through many stages to get to where it is today. We focus on helping people to secure their future, and live their dreams – Financial Planning.

We also help them to manage their assets with professional investment advice – Investment Management.

Along the way, in addition to the legal examinations I have qualified as a Certified Financial Planner (CFP$^{CM}$). This is a high-level, international qualification which trains advisers to become financial planners. We focus on the practical skills necessary to deliver a comprehensive financial plan which helps people to achieve their goals rather than sell them products. I am also a Chartered Wealth Manager (Chartered MSCI), which is a top-level investment advice qualification.

# Why I wrote this book

## My philosophy

My Financial Planning philosophy has been shaped by my story. My personal and professional experiences have led me to the point where I have a clear vision of how things should be. I think of my role in clients' lives as being a guide through the complex world of finances. This can be incredibly complicated but using experience I can get people to understand the core aspects of an idea. When people can see the core idea they can more easily take action.

## We are all headed in one direction

The harsh reality of my mum's story is that we know we are all going to die one day. We don't like to think about it but we know it's true. We are faced with this reality on a regular basis but we often put these thoughts aside and focus on living our day to day lives. I want to challenge you to think about your mortality in a positive way. The rest of the time you have left in the world is precious, so you'd better make the most of it. You need to take time to think about the future rather than just the present.

The problem we all face is that we don't know how long we have left. My mum didn't know she would die when she was 50. If she had, she might have lived her life differently. Of course, this doesn't mean you need to live your life for the here and now. You still need to plan for the future, and this book will help you to do that.

The problem that many people face is that they think they have a lot of time left. This thinking leads you to delay taking action and means you can end up sleep-walking into a future you didn't plan and didn't want.

## We need to know when to stop

You work hard and see that as a way to provide security for yourself and your family. Of course, that's right, but how will you know when will be the right time to stop?

### Bill's story

Bill's story is probably familiar to you. Bill worked hard for 45 years, got to 65, was given a farewell party at his office, received his carriage clock and left to retire with a pension of sorts. Bill put off his dreams, thinking that he could have plenty of time to do all that when he retired. He planned to visit all those places he never had the time or money to see when he was working. He wanted to play golf every day. Unfortunately, Bill didn't get to live his dreams because he died a few months after retirement.

Both Bill's story and my mum's story tell me that life can change very quickly. It's difficult to be sure when to stop working and start doing what you really want with life. I hope this book will help you with that. My philosophy is that if you have enough (and you can prove to yourself you have enough) then you should stop working and start doing what you really want with your life.

You may think that working is what really motivates you. If that is the case, you may never want to stop working. That's brilliant if that's what you really want. I see a lot of people, particularly business owners, who forget why they started to work so hard in the first place. If you can understand what really motivates you, then you can set some priorities and put the work and the money into perspective. You should think hard about what is important to you outside of work and money. When you think back on your life do you ever think 'I wish I had worked more weekends'?

### Live your dreams

If life can be short and brutal then you need to live the fullest life you can, while you are still fit and able to do so. You owe it to yourself and your family to think this way. Don't let yourself be lured into the trap that you can work hard now and it will all come good in the end. You need to recognise what's important to you and your family both now and in the future. This starts with securing your future. Security brings you the ability to live your dreams.

You probably do not care about the financial products you hold. What you care about is what that money can do for you and your family. More importantly, you need to put that money to work for you to live the life you want. I hate it when I see people sitting on piles of cash because they don't have the vision to know how to spend it, or they are too scared of running out one day. You'd be amazed how often I see people sitting on hundreds of thousands of pounds in savings and investments who live frugal existences. Of course, the frugal habits were probably what led them to build up these assets in the first place, but not to use that money seems a pity and a waste. Often they are held back by the fear of lack of security. We try to show them how much they will need so they can be sure they will never run out of money. Hopefully, this book will help you to realise this too. The rest can be put to use to live your dreams.

## Why do people put off Financial Planning?

If you delay planning your finances you are less likely to achieve your goals. You are less likely to achieve the security you crave, and even less likely to live your dreams.

Don't be put off by what has gone before – that is gone. You can only focus on the future, and make small changes towards your long-term vision. These changes, applied regularly and consistently, will make your dreams much more likely to happen.

Here are some reasons why people put off Financial Planning. Think honestly about your own experience and work out if any of these reasons have held you back. This book will get you started on overcoming all these issues.

## I'm far too busy

Of course you are. We all are. This doesn't mean you shouldn't plan your finances. If you're genuinely too busy, just bite the bullet and pay someone like me to do it for you. The reality is that while you're busy doing something urgent, something important like planning your future is slipping by.

There's a great analysis of this problem in The *7 habits of highly effective people* by Stephen Covey (see **7figuresplan.com/resources**). Dr Covey describes people furiously cutting down trees, being busy at what they do. What you should really do is climb a tall tree and work out if you're in the right forest to begin with. A financial plan will give you that direction, and then you can get back to cutting down the trees that will genuinely help you more forwards.

## I don't know where to look for information

All the information you need is out there in books, websites, blogs, newspapers, videos, podcasts and other formats. You just need to find the trustworthy sources and start the process of learning for yourself.

It is a poor excuse to say that you don't know where to look for information. We live in the best time ever to be alive. The world is awash with technology and information. This can seem daunting, but there are some fantastic resources available which will get you started on your journey towards financial freedom.

Obviously, you have taken a great step by picking up this book as it is a summary and simplification of some of the most important Financial Planning themes.

There is nothing really new in this book. All I have done is to assemble the elements you need and to simplify things in a way which will help you to start to take action. By the way, I recommend a series of resources for you to review at the end of this book if you want some guidance as to where to start looking for more information. You can also check out **7figuresplan.com/resources**

## It's too complicated

Financial Planning *is* too complicated and I believe that most financial institutions and many advisers go out of their way to keep it that way. Many financial products are complicated, but often there are very good reasons for this.

Don't let the fact that Financial Planning can be complicated become an excuse for inaction. It is your responsibility to address this issue head on. No-one else will do it for you, and why should they? Financial Planning and financial products can be complicated but the fundamental principles and core concepts do not need to be. What is contained in this book is quite simple, and I have deliberately kept it that way. I will give you the basic tools so you can take action now on the things that are important to your financial security. Just because it can be complicated does not mean that you can avoid taking action. Otherwise you may condemn yourself and your family to a harder life than you need to.

## I just want quick results

There is a serious problem with how the media portrays successful people. This has hoodwinked us all into thinking that the solution to our financial woes is some sort of quick fix. The reality is that it is extremely rare for people to get rich quickly. Most people who have 'made it' got there extremely slowly because they have built up the skills necessary to make money and grow their assets.

Think about anyone who is famous: perhaps a talented star, or some sort of business leader. Almost all of them got there through consistent hard work over many, many years by perfecting their skills. They did not give up when doors were slammed in their face, and they learned from these experiences. They did not expect to get rich quickly. Those who do get rich quickly rarely last the course, and often lose their money because they didn't build the skills necessary to keep their money growing. I'm sure you have read stories of big lottery winners who lost it all. Usually that's because they didn't learn the skills to make and keep the money.

The media loves to tell us about these people who were extremely lucky because they are so rare. I am sorry to tell you that if you are reading this book you are not going to get lucky and you are not going to win the lottery. If you want results they are going to have to come slowly, and over time unless you are prepared to take some calculated risks.

### I just want someone to tell me what to do

I see this a lot, and we have built our business on the back of this. If you have money to start with then this is probably a viable option. All of our clients are capable of following the principles in this book. Most of them come to us because they do not have the time or inclination to follow these principles. They value their time and want to focus on living their dreams. They prefer to pay us to ensure that they remain secure and they avoid any costly mistakes.

Despite this even our clients cannot abdicate responsibility for understanding how their future is going to be. We educate our clients on the principles in this book because they need that understanding of the core concepts to be able to make decisions on their future.

If you lack understanding about basic financial principles then you run the risk of being bamboozled into taking action against your interests. By making the excuse that you want someone to tell you what to do you run many risks. You could be taken advantage of by some charlatan, or worse still a well-meaning fool. Believe me, they still exist, despite significant regulation. You also leave yourself open to taking the advice of people who have limited investment in your success.

## I can't afford it

Unfortunately, this is a reality of the modern world. Although we earn more than previous generations, modern life still seems to suck all of our resources and money. The reality is that you can afford to plan for your future; you just need to understand your priorities. Following the plan in this book will help you to understand where your money goes. Armed with this information you will be able to prioritise your spending and begin to afford to pay for what is most important to you and your family.

This problem is not confined to those on limited incomes. I often see people on significant incomes who spend everything (and more) of what they earn. These high expenses leave them with the same limited disposable incomes as those on lower salaries.

So, it is all about priorities. You probably can afford it, but you just need to want it enough. Don't make the mistake of telling yourself that you can't afford it. This will just lead you down the path of inaction.

## I can't see past the short-term

This is a genuine difficulty for many (or even most) people. It is hard to think past your immediate life, and especially 20 or 30 years into the future. Financial planning is about time travel – to visualise how your life should be in the future and build a plan backwards from there to create a plan of action in the present to make that dream a reality. It is difficult to force yourself to work on your future self. If you follow the principles of this book you will start to work on this skill. The results will come in the end.

You are bombarded with advertising messages of how to make your life better now. That's the job of marketing – to get you to take action that is designed to improve your life now. Financial Planning is all about delayed gratification, which can be difficult when confronted with the pressures of life. Financial Planning will help you to take action which will benefit you in the future. If you are concerned about leading a secure and fulfilling life then you need to think about the long-term as well as the short-term. You can't afford to make the mistake of just looking at the short-term. The result will be a less fulfilling life later on, as you'll have less time to work on your future.

### *Logic v emotion*

Our brains are programmed to work both logically and emotionally. We think we are rational individuals who take all decisions based on logical assessments of facts. The reality is that almost all of our decisions are made on auto pilot. These decisions are taken by the emotional part of our brain.

The emotional part of our brain helps us to take quick decisions based on our instincts. Think about it. When you stand in line to buy a sandwich, do you consider all the relative merits of the various choices in front of you, their calorie counts and the energy to price ratio? No, you probably go for something like you always have done. This is the emotional part of your brain in action, and it works well to stop analysis paralysis. We are faced with thousands of decisions every day, and we need to take quick action on all of them. If you stop to think through every choice you would probably not leave the house in the morning.

The logical part of our brain takes the considered decisions, and analyses the situation based on the evidence available. You engage the logical part sparingly when you need to focus on some sort of analysis. The problem is that this is not necessarily your default choice when coming to a quick decision. The emotional part of your brain does not let the logical part come to the fore when the pressure is on.

Is it better to listen to logic or emotion when making strategic decisions about your future? Be honest with yourself - has emotion sometimes guided some of your financial decisions?

Let's take an example. We all know we should take regular exercise. Sometimes we even get inspired to sign up to a class, or join a gym. The logical part of your brain takes control and rejoices in your plan of action. Of course, the emotional part also took a part in the decision making process as you probably needed it to make a decision. The logical side creates an eating plan, an exercise plan, and you sign up to an expensive gym contract committing you to taking action.

The emotional part takes over when it starts to hurt or you get cravings for chocolate. You rationalise certain emotional decisions, saying that having one doughnut won't hurt, or missing one exercise session won't make a difference. Of course, taken alone this is certainly true – I don't know anyone who has died as a result of missing a session at the gym. But the reality is that over time the decisions taken on emotion will have an effect. You will fall out of the good habits you should follow, and start to follow far less effective habits. Over time this will mean you do not live your dreams.

Think about how this could apply to your life in a financial sense. Let's say your nine year old daughter wants a pony. I reckon that on being presented with this request the logical side of your brain will be screaming 'No!!!' as it will be calculating the immense costs and commitment of such an involvement, realising that in the end the child might not want to continue with this hobby. But your child, master of manipulation, will break down your resistance with emotional appeals. If emotion wins, you'll be committed to a significant financial outlay, which could impact on other logical longer-term goals such as saving for your daughter's university fees.

I do not want you to think that the emotion should never win. One of your dreams might be to buy your daughter a pony. In this case, you should engage the logical side of your brain to make this happen. You could produce a way for yourself to be able to afford the pony without impacting on other longer-term goals and dreams. You can then have the pleasure of giving this wonderful gift to your daughter without an impact on your future security.

This applies to your life in many ways, not just financial. This book is designed to help you avoid making too many costly emotional mistakes.

### I can't trust financial institutions

There is a pervading cynicism because financial crises have undermined trust in financial services. This is completely valid, since financial and political institutions tend to put short-term profits above all else. In some ways our financial system is fundamentally flawed on a systemic level. Despite this I do not want cynicism to hold back your own planning. You owe it to yourself and your family to live the fullest life you can. Financial Planning will help you to do that, so you need to understand the issues which are most relevant to you and focus on these. This knowledge will enable you to manage the manipulations and pressures of financial institutions. Ultimately, this can help you to get to your goals faster, unencumbered by the marketing. Just trust in your own financial decisions.

# What you will get from this book

How do you overcome all the reasons against beginning your Financial Plan? This book will be a good starting point for you in the following ways.

# A step-by-step approach

The most important aspect of this book is that you will gain a step-by-step approach, including materials, which you can use immediately. You will be able to follow the method and apply it to your own financial life and use it to develop your own dreams. The ideas and guidance are designed to be practical and easy to use. You do not need any prior financial experience; you just need to follow your own common sense.

Some aspects are more advanced, and I will flag these up along the way. This will help you to know if these issues affect you, and you will be able to recognise that you might require further advice or assistance.

You will be left with a practical plan. The 7 figures plan will identify and address the areas of your finances which require the most immediate action.

## Visualise your future

You need to understand what you want from life by looking over the horizon towards your future. This can be difficult to do, but such insight will motivate you and help you to decide on your direction of travel.

## Knowledge of what is really important

I really want to give you the ability to focus on what is *really* important in your Financial Planning. The financial world can seem overly complex to many people, so I want you to be able to distil this down to some vital principles, which will put you along the path to security and living your dreams. You will use these to choose your strategy.

There will be other issues addressed along the way, where these are relevant, but the overall focus will be on the most important elements, which will deliver the greatest results.

## Take action

This book is not going to solve all your financial woes overnight. It will not make you financially independent immediately. It will instead inspire you to take action. I believe that you should be taking the small steps day by day, week by week, year by year, which will all add up to a powerful journey towards your security and ultimately living your dreams.

If you do not take action now, you need to be prepared to settle for less later on. This book will show you how to take action, and where the best results can be achieved.

## The fundamentals, not products

In the past, the financial advice industry has focussed too much on products and features – that's how they earned their money. The Financial Planning movement changed this focus to examine the fundamental principles first. This is based on sound principles, which we all know but do not always apply. The products may be important, and can obviously solve certain financial problems. Despite this, you can not genuinely know whether you need a financial product until you conduct some sort of comprehensive financial analysis of your goals, your current situation and the gap between the two. Only then can you be sure that you need a financial product.

This is how I see the process working:

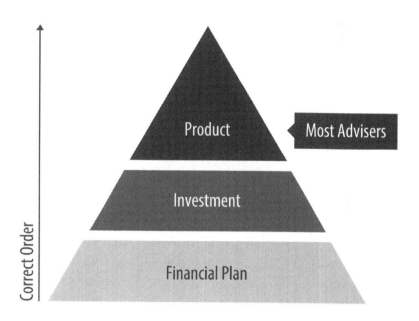

The financial plan you will create as a result of this book is the foundation of your future, the basis on which the pyramid above is built. I believe that you must focus your time on this area before all others, or risk serious miscalculations in the other areas in the future.

Of secondary importance are your investments. This is a technical area worthy of its own book, but I believe that you can only take investment decisions once you have a direction from your financial plan. For example, you may decide that you are prepared to take moderate risks with your investments. That is fine on the surface, but what if your financial plan reveals that to achieve the security you want and the dreams you have set you actually need to be *more* adventurous with your investments? What if your dreams are so unrealistic that wild risks need to be taken with investments to have any chance of success?

The solution might be to take more risk; or if you are not prepared to do that you might decide to work longer, earn more or reduce your dreams.

The reverse might be true. What if your financial plan showed that you are prepared to take moderate risks, but that to achieve your goals you do not need to take any risks? In general, if you do not need to take risks then you should not – only take as much risk as is required to meet your goals, so that you are more likely to achieve them. Instead, you might decide that you *can* take moderate risk but by doing so you can bring forward your goals, or make your goals bigger. Who is not in favour of living bigger goals?

The product, while important, is the area which requires least attention. This is because the fundamental aspects of your financial plan (and your investments) will drive the reasons for the product. Your financial analysis might show that you do not actually need a product. Many financial products are complex, and require financial advice. At least by following the principles of this book you will be in a stronger position to decide what you actually need.

You should be following the direction of the vertical arrow. Start by examining fundamental principles so you can see the big picture. From there you can manage risk versus reward. Finally, take action or implement a solution, but *only if this is needed*. Be wary of "advisers" who start with the solutions and products. If they go straight for the solution, they run the risk of missing something more important in your fundamental Financial Planning. Perhaps they don't have your best interests at heart...

## Straightforward, not technical

The processes recommended in this book are deliberately straightforward. There are often technical reasons behind these processes, but I do not believe you need to know all these to start a plan of action. By all means investigate further if this interests you. You can use the resources I have flagged up.

Therefore, you will be glad to learn that there is limited technical information in this book unless it is strictly necessary to aid understanding. I want to give you the practical tools you need to know to enable you to start some real change in your current and future financial planning.

# Why make a financial plan?

## Focus on the fundamentals

Your financial plan examines all the fundamental best practices to build a solid foundation for your future security. By doing this you will have a better understanding and analysis of the gaps in your planning so that you allocate your resources in the most appropriate way.

## Longer-term planning

Financial Planning allows you to think into your future. I like to call it time travel since it encourages you to consider what your own life will be in the distant future. Financial Planning is a process that allows you to examine what your future should be in the best possible scenario, and then to work backwards from there to the present. By doing this you will be able to work out a plan of action to take now, with the aim of securing your future and living the best life you can.

## Security

Financial Security is the most important issue for almost everyone. It is what drives most of our financial actions, and can often be a powerful motivation. This desire for security can be destructive, because if it exists alongside a lack of clarity you may unwittingly work too long, take too little risk, or sit on cash which could be better spent living a better life.

Why do people think this way? It is natural to worry about your future and whether the money will run out. For many people the fear of loss is much greater than the drive towards gain. This is why we buy fixed rate mortgages, or keep money in savings accounts when the returns are behind inflation.

I like to tell a story about the day when my wife found £10 outside a department store. We looked around for anyone to claim it and found no-one. Happy we had done our bit, we promptly marched into the closest café and treated ourselves to coffees and cakes, toasting her good fortune. It was a nice feeling, but lasted about an hour. Imagine if she had lost £10. The feeling of loss would have lasted far beyond the time it took to munch through those cakes! She would have been complaining for a lot longer.

Most people would feel worse at losing this money than the positive feeling you might have if you found an equivalent amount.

The need for security is a powerful desire in all of us. For this reason, your financial plan needs to be geared up to provide security first. Only once you are sure that you are secure can you push on to work towards your bigger, fulfilling dreams. If you fear for your security then you may hold back your other goals and dreams. This is a real shame as it puts at risk your responsibility to live the best life you can.

I even see this with clients who pay me to work with them on their Financial Planning. Even though they have paid an expert to examine their situation, they often remain cautious in making decisions since they cannot quite believe the evidence in front of them.

## Control

The concept of control is linked to security. I often see people who have enough money to live the life they want. They are never in danger of running out of money no matter what happens. You would think that they would start to use their excess assets, perhaps to help out their family. They don't take this action, partly due to a fear of losing security, but also out of a sense of a need to keep control over those assets just in case something happens.

Financial Planning allows you to examine different scenarios so that you can be confident that you will have control over your life no matter what happens. These scenarios could cover disaster situations, low investment growth, redundancy or anything else you might want to consider.

# Achieve your goals faster

If you focus on your goals you are much more likely to achieve them. If you write them down and regularly review them you are even more likely to get to where you want to be. Financial Planning is a process that you can use to achieve your goals faster. It will allow you to focus on what is important to you now and in the future so that you are less likely to get distracted by things that don't matter. Your financial plan will allow you to keep on track towards your goals. Just by taking regular action you will achieve your goals faster than you realise.

# Cover all the major issues

Financial Planning is a process that forces you to cover all the major issues which affect everyone. Of course, some of these issues will not apply to your individual situation. If this is the case all you need to do is adapt the process to suit you. However, do this at your peril since experience tells me that nearly all of the themes covered in this book should apply to most people.

By going through the process of Financial Planning you will be sure that you have covered all the bases. You can then use this to provide the security you probably crave. Once this has been achieved you can start to live the dreams you build. Not only will you be able to cover all the major issues that could affect you during your financial journey, but you will also be able to prioritise them. This is very important since this focus will help you to allocate your resources in a logical way rather than all over the place. This focus will enable you to get to where you want to go faster.

### Issues covered by a financial plan

These are some of the major themes addressed by using the Financial Planning process:

1. Life expectancy
   Medical science is a remarkable thing. It has advanced so far that we all expect to live much longer lives than even just a few generations ago. This is a wonderful thing, but it does raise the thorny issue that we have to be able to pay for these extra years. The traditional pattern of work surely has to change since it is no longer feasible to work for 40 years and then retire for 20-30 years. At least this is true if you have not done some serious Financial Planning along the way.

   If you want a traditional comfortable retirement, you need to put aside more than you could imagine.

2. The State cannot afford to provide for you
   The State will have to shrink from its provision to you. Leaving aside the debt problems affecting most Western societies, the problem has become one of demographics. In the past, the State provided a basic retirement fund for you (the State Pension) using contributions from the working population to pay for the retirement of older people. Now, the ratio of working taxpayers to retired is reducing, so that eventually we might move from 3 people working to 1 retired, to 1 working for 1 retired. There are more and more retired people, and there are not enough working people to pay State benefits for them. You can see this in action in the UK with State pensions being pushed back from 60 or 65 to 66, 67 and 68. I do not see an end to this, so my message is that you cannot rely on the State too much.

   You can't rely on the State and need to start making your own provision for your future security.

3. Savings habit
   It seems that we earn more than ever before in comparison to previous generations, but the cost of living increases with our

desire to want more out of life. Along the way, the savings habit has been severely eroded so that many people are only a few weeks away from disaster if they lost their job due to redundancy or illness. The savings habit is what is going to provide you with future security, and the sooner you start and accelerate your work on this regard, the sooner you will be able to secure your future. The only alternative to saving is to earn more instead. This book should give you a good idea of how much you need to put aside.

4. Sickness and death

You need to look at disaster planning to be sure that your family's standard of living can continue should the worst happen. The State can really only afford to provide you with subsistence in these scenarios, so you need to be able to survive on your own should the worst happen. Most people put some plans into force to pay off their mortgage debt if they die, but few think about more likely scenarios of serious illness along the way. Most people also fail to think about how their family would pay the normal household bills in these situations.

What the State can afford to provide you in a disaster situation will not be enough.

5. Tax

Not many people are delighted to pay tax. Of course, tax is a fact of life for us all. We all need roads, schools and hospitals. But you need to start looking at tax as one of your expenditure items. For many people it is difficult to reduce their tax bill. However, you need to understand the relationship that tax has with your spending, and this shift in your thinking may alter how you approach certain issues. The reality is that tax forms something between 25% and 50% of your spending. You just do not necessarily see it on a day to day basis.

You must understand how tax impacts your expenditure.

6. Debt

   Debt seems to be a fact of life for most of us. Debt forms a significant part of this book since it is one of the biggest things that holds back your future financial prosperity. The debt mountain that we build up as individuals seems to be growing year by year. But only by becoming debt-free can you be truly financially free. I realise that there can be a more nuanced view than this, and I will explore this theme in later chapters, but my overall message is that your debts are someone else's assets.

   Aim to become debt-free as soon as you can.

# Work out how much is enough

This is a difficult question to answer for most people. Many people work too long because they do not know how much is enough to live the life they want and never run out of money. They keep working and keep accumulating since they want and crave security in their life. This drives them to work harder, spending longer hours at work. They also tend to work for years past when they may have already been financially free. I want to help you on the path towards working out how much is really enough to live the life you want. This figure is important since it will help you to work out when you can stop accumulating and start spending. Of course, that does not mean you have to stop work. It just means that you have the ability to stop if that is what you want.

## *Financial independence*

Knowledge of this figure is important because it tells you when you have become financially independent. Financial independence is the ability to be able to live off your assets and not have to work. This means having enough in income producing assets to fund your current and future lifestyle needs. You can use income and capital to achieve these goals.

Financial independence does not mean that you have to hang up your boots and sit in a darkened room. What it gives you is the freedom to decide your future. You can choose to work if that is what motivates you. You can choose to focus on other things that are important to you such as:

- Family
- A new challenge
- Hobbies and interests
- Charity or community work
- Your health
- Your spirituality
- Another business or job
- Learning new skills

The choice is up to you, but financial independence will give you the opportunity to explore these opportunities on your terms. By the way, I am not saying that you should wait until you are financially free to explore these issues. You have the ability to focus on them now, but by knowing how much is enough one day you will be financially free to devote as much time as you want to these themes.

# Key drivers to success in your Financial Planning

Before you start on your financial plan I want to share with you what is going to be required to achieve success with your goals. Reading this book is not going to be enough. You must take action, and you must not put this off. Every day you put off taking any action, however small, means a delay in achieving financial security. Inaction means delaying living your dreams.

If you are not prepared to take these actions then you should probably put this book down. You then have 2 choices:

1. <u>Resign yourself to not achieving future financial security</u> (and therefore not living your dreams); **or**
2. <u>Find yourself a Financial Planner</u> (and be prepared to pay for their services – see Chapter 9)

Hiring a Financial Planner is a short-cut to getting to where you want, because you can pay someone who understands all the major issues covered by this book. They will work with you to keep you on the path to achieving your goals. The pay-off is the cost of their services, but at least you know that you should avoid costly mistakes along the way. If you do not have the time or inclination to learn about Financial Planning yourself then this is the logical step to take. I explore this issue in more detail later in the book, so if you get to the end and think that hiring a Financial Planner is right for you, I provide a blueprint for how to find the right one for you. By the way, hiring a good Financial Planner is not necessarily the easy option. You will still need to do a lot of work, and they will challenge you to consider your decisions. A good Financial Planner will embark on a programme of education with you to ensure that you are equipped to make the financial decisions necessary.

## What is required to achieve success in your financial plan?

### Write your plan down

There have been many studies that show that if you write a plan down you are much more likely to use the plan on a regular basis, and are therefore much more likely to achieve your goals. Of course, you also need to actually look at the plan on a regular basis. You need to develop the habits necessary to drive action. This is why this book focusses on making your plan as simple as possible so that you focus only on the key drivers to success.

### Involve someone else

This is extremely important since it will force your plan to become real.

If you have the courage to outline your future plans to someone else then this will make you accountable to yourself and them. You would be surprised how motivating this can be. You need to schedule regular appointments with this person to ensure that you keep reviewing your progress. Again, this element is about holding you to account for your goals and dreams. If you keep your plans to yourself you need to be extremely motivated over a long period of time. I would suggest that this is unlikely to be sustainable forever. Involving someone else in your financial plan makes you accountable and keeps you motivated.

So who should you involve in your financial plan? Well, the choice is yours, but I would suggest any or all of the following.

- Your partner
  You should involve your partner or spouse, since many of the decisions taken will involve them. I would go further to suggest that they should be involved at every stage since you may not have discussed such weighty issues in the past, at least to any significant degree. It is likely that you share some similarities with your partner regarding many of the issues covered in this book. However, there are likely to be differences in how you approach many of the possible solutions. Your approach to risk and your priorities regarding your goals and dreams are likely to be quite different. Do not make the mistake of assuming that your views are the same. The more you discuss these issues with your partner then the bigger the likelihood that you will achieve a harmonious future for you both.

  If you involve your partner in your financial plan on a regular basis you will also be able to share the load. The process should be more fun and more motivating as a result. You can also avoid conflicts where certain behaviours or spending patterns can be avoided which do not fit into the ultimate goals.

  I apply this on a regular basis in my own family life. All my financial decisions are taken together with my wife (who is also my business partner). We have an agreed plan for the short-term and long-term so that we take financial decisions together within the confines of this arrangement. What this means is that financial issues are never a source of conflict between us since we both understand the bigger picture. We can take bigger decisions in the context of the overall plan, meaning that we are less likely to be taken off track by short-term desires or emotional decisions. If we do change the short-term direction we do so in the knowledge of how this impacts the longer-term goals. More importantly, we hold each other to account and keep each other motivated. It is a powerful thing.

- <u>Other confidantes</u>
  You could share your financial plans with any other trusted person. This could be a friend or a coach or mentor. It really does not matter who you share your plans with, so long as they share your vision for your future and work with you to get there. You want to choose someone who will not hold you back since they will have a significant influence on your decisions and your motivation. They will also be a great source of inspiration by recommending other sources of learning.

By the way, I apply this in my personal and professional life too. We have a business coach and a fitness coach. We use both people as a trusted mentor to help to keep us moving towards our declared goals. They both help to keep us on the course we have set so that we are much more likely to keep taking the small steps necessary to achieving our various goals. By constantly keeping to the agreed process we have set we remain accountable to ourselves and stay motivated. I know that when I work with these coaches I achieve far more than I would do alone, because I keep my focus.

- Financial planner

  You should share your plan with your Financial Planner, if you have one. They will be in a prime position to give you practical and technical guidance on the issues in this book. I hope that they will agree with how we have guided you!

## *Keep learning*

It is not enough to read this book. This book merely gives you the framework so you can build your financial plan. You must commit yourself to constant self-improvement, in whichever way suits you. There is a vast array of excellent financial resources out there. You just need to find those which suit your own needs and how you see the world.

### New ideas

Constant learning brings a ready source of new ideas. The world is constantly changing and finance is definitely at the forefront of change. The issues covered in this book are fundamental but the decisions you make as a result will depend on the technical products and rules at the time. You need to be open to new ideas on a regular basis so that you do not fall behind what you need to know. You will need to build on your existing knowledge to help you to make better financial decisions. As you expose yourself to a regular stream of new ideas and concepts you may start to make more effective decisions. You will also learn from those who have put in the hard work and have already made the mistakes so you do not have to.

### Sharpen your skills

Constant learning will sharpen your financial skills in ways you cannot predict. Your decisions will become clearer, quicker and more effective. Your mistakes will be fewer and less important since you will be learning and applying from those who have made and avoided these mistakes. Remember, there is little out there that is completely new, but that does not necessarily mean that you know about it. Therefore, you should embark on a journey of constant self-improvement. I promise that you will not regret it.

Suggested resources

There is an amazing array of free and low-cost learning material out there. The only challenge is to find the sources that you can trust, and find the time to learn from the materials and apply it. Here are some suggested types of resources you could look up. The medium you use is up to your particular learning style.

- Books
  There are thousands of financial planning titles to choose from. You do not even have to limit yourself to purely financial texts. Just find the subjects that interest you and look them up online. Getting feedback from customer reviews is easy, and of course you can consume this material in traditional form or electronically. I have always got a self-development book on the go, and I will never catch up on my reading list because I am always keeping the list up to date when others recommend titles to me. Personally, I prefer to buy traditional books since I can make my own notes directly on the text. This helps me to consolidate my learning as I go. Whichever way you look at it, is it not worth spending a few pounds to get the lifetime learning of an expert in their field?

  The way I do it is to maintain a "Wish List" on my Amazon account. This helps me to keep a central resource of possible titles to read so that I can always keep one on the go. You don't have to buy from Amazon, although of course they make it easy.

  Go to **7figuresplan.com/resources** for a full list of recommended further reading titles.

- Websites and newsletters
  You really do not have to go far to find trustworthy sources. This information tends to be current in its form, so you need to balance the need for up to date information versus a focus on the fundamental issues. Many websites have free or low-cost learning materials for you to broaden your knowledge in specific subjects. You can use these materials to build on the topics contained in this book. You can often sign up to the mailing lists of many sites so that you get a regular stream of information on subjects you are interested in. Just remember, the journalistic standards online may be different to printed media. Be aware that there could be ulterior motives behind the published content you are reading.

  The way I do it is to use RSS feeds. Most websites with regularly updated content will also publish this in an RSS feed. You can use this in conjunction with a feed reader to access information on particular topics when you want it. You can sort your sources by the subjects you are interested in, and access the updates when suitable.

  Go to **7figuresplan.com/resources** to find more recommended resources.

- Newspapers and magazines
  Most quality titles have a finance section either daily or weekly. This can be a good source of current financial information. There are also magazines which focus on financial issues. The articles will be well-written and are usually considered. The only downside is that by their nature these articles tend to be topical in nature. Journalists do not need to be financially qualified, although they are usually knowledgeable. The major issue for me is that the newspapers tend to look at what is current rather than what fundamentally works. For me, you are much more

likely to get a good overview of the fundamentals in a book like this one.

I recommend that you get a good quality broadsheet newspaper every weekend so that you can keep current with financial issues in the press.

- Videos
  Videos can be a really accessible form of financial education. You can find videos on any subject you want via websites mentioned above, or on platforms such as YouTube. If visual learning is your style then this is probably for you. Just a word of warning – I tend to find that the content published by many financial institutions is extremely technical and dull. Look out for those sites which publish practical "how-to" videos, since these can help you to accelerate learning in complex areas.

- Audiobooks, podcasts and radio
  Personally, I love audio since I can consume it while I am doing other activities such as driving or going to the gym. You can access financial information from sources such as mainstream radio, or specialist podcasts. I use a podcast application on my smartphone to download episodes (for free) from a variety of sources. I can then listen to them days or weeks later at my convenience.

You can also buy books in audio format. This is a great way to keep learning, although it can be difficult to take notes while you are driving!

Go to **7figuresplan.com/resources** for more resources in this area.

- Social Media
  You can use the social media platforms of your choice to follow trusted sources of financial education. They will probably post tips and links to information on current topics of interest. Again, you can use this to access information when you want it.

  You can link with me on social media here:
  **7figuresplan.com/social**

## Chapter summary

- The time you have left is your most valuable resource
- We all need to know when to stop accumulating
- Most people crave security before they will work on living their dreams
- There are many reasons not to plan your finances – don't put it off any longer
- Visualise your future to give you focus and gain knowledge of what is important
- The only way to make change is to start taking action
- Focus on the fundamentals and don't worry about financial products
- Cover all the major issues and you will be closer to financial security
- You will be financially independent when you have enough to stop working if that's your choice
- If you want to be successful with Financial Planning you should write your plan down, involve someone else to hold you to account, and keep learning
- If you're not prepared to do the work, be prepared to fail, or hire a Financial Planner

# Chapter 2 - The 7 figures you need to know

So now we are starting to get to the stage in this book where I will lay out the practical aspects of the 7 Figures plan. This is a practical and straightforward method to help you understand the 7 key figures you need to know to be able to create enough focus to start to take action in your financial planning.

## The 7 Figures Plan concept

### Time travel

The 7 Figures plan will turn you into a time traveller. Unfortunately, you don't get to drive a De Lorien or battle Darleks from your Tardis. The 7 Figures Plan allows you to look into your future and work backwards from there to today. If you can take the difficult step and examine what your future should be like, then you can work this back to the actions you need to take now to get to where you want to be. Failure to do this means leaving your future up to chance. Building a plan will help you to get to the future you want.

This time travel allows you to examine various future scenarios based on assumptions about the way things could come about. This helps you to avoid certain problems and risks. You will also make important decisions based on a proper examination of the alternatives. If you can map out the implications of taking (or not taking) a certain course of action, then you can use this knowledge to work out which course of action is right for you. You will do this based on some scientific principles rather than hoping for the best.

## Long-term rather than day to day

The 7 Figures Plan is about examining the long-term direction you are taking. You will set your decisions in to context and set some priorities for action. If you do not take the time to examine your future, you are much less likely to see the results you want in the long-term. Therefore, you will examine your long-term goals before you look at your day to day actions. Of course, the analysis you make will start to change your day to day behaviours.

## Sensible decisions

The 7 Figures Plan gets you to make sensible decisions based on logic rather than emotion. You will follow a process to make quicker and smarter decisions about your future and your current situation.

We want you to use logic to control your strategic financial decisions. Emotional decisions will always be there, but we need to moderate this influence so you always make these in the context of the big picture you set for yourself.

## *A simple plan*

Financial decisions do not have to be overly complicated. Yes, I realise that financial issues can be extremely complex, especially when you start to think about products, tax and other issues. However, at their heart, most financial decisions can be reduced to straightforward common sense. If you have a good grasp of the fundamentals then you will be well-equipped to create a plan that works.

## Focus on the important bits

The 7 Figures Plan is a way for you to focus on the important bits first. You can examine more complicated issues later and with the help of experts if necessary. Gaining a grasp of the fundamental issues gives you clarity over your situation. This leads to a better chance of making good decisions.

<u>A way to take action and see results</u>

Once you will have a straightforward overview of your situation you will be able to start to take action immediately. The biggest reason that people fail in their financial planning is because they fail to take action. There are many reasons why you might fail to take action. The 7 Figures Plan is a process you can use to strip away these excuses for inaction. When you are left with your simple plan you are much more likely to begin to take the necessary actions to lead towards your future security. These actions will ultimately lead you to living your dreams whatever they may be.

A simple plan leads to clarity in your finances. Clarity leads to understanding. This understanding leads to action. Action leads to results. It is that simple.

## Anyone can do it

You do not need to have any qualifications or experience to take the action necessary to secure your future and live your dreams. You just need the commitment to follow through the concepts in this book and to apply them on a regular basis. Remember that the principles in this book are straightforward and common sense. To be honest, you probably already know most of them, but whether you are applying them is another matter. Knowledge is nothing without action. The 7 Figures Plan will help you to take action.

## What are the 7 key Figures in your plan?

The 7 Figures Plan is not only about the 7 key figures mentioned below. It is also about the *relationship* between these key figures. You will focus on understanding the nature of these areas, and then work on ways to apply this knowledge to create action towards your ultimate goals.

### Figure 1 - your age now

The first key figure in your plan is your current age. You need to examine where you are and where you have been in the past. You should not focus too much on the past because that is gone, but you need to place your plan into the context of where you are now against the future goals you will set.

You need to recognise the truth of your current position, as this will have an effect on your ability to work on changes in the future.

### Figure 2 - the age you will stop accumulating

The age you stop accumulating will directly affect all other areas of your planning. This will determine how much time you need to rely on the assets you generate over your lifetime, and will therefore impact on how much is enough to live the life you want without running out of money.

You will need to be realistic about this stage, but also think about the goals and dreams you have for the future. In many ways, this is the most important part of the 7 Figures Plan.

Imagine you are sitting in a boat, which is a way of thinking about your lifetime journey. Your boat is currently in the middle of the ocean. From this point, you could go in many different directions, so you it will help you greatly if you can think about a destination for your journey, which is where the boat will come to rest. Your life will continue after that but in a different way. Your past decisions may mean that you have not made much progress towards your final destination. In addition, the size of your ambitions will determine how far you have left to travel, and how much work will be required to get you to your destination.

### Figure 3 - income

Your income is the money you have coming in to your household from various sources, both now and in the future. This is extremely important since your income is the driver of all other aspects of your plan. Think of your income as the engine room of your 7 Figures Plan. Without an income of a sufficient size you will not be able to generate enough money to plan for your future.

Think of your boat as having 2 propellers. The first is powered manually and by you working hard to generate enough momentum to move forward. Your income determines how much effort you can divert to moving your boat forward. If you have a large income you can power the boat faster in this way. The second propeller is powered by your assets (see Figure 5 below)

## Figure 4 - expenditure

Your expenditure is closely related to your income. Your expenditure is important because it governs the lifestyle you lead both now and in the future. Obviously, you cannot exist in the modern world without spending money. Therefore, you need to understand where your money goes.

Why is this important? If you can spend less than you earn you will have some surplus to put towards your future security, and living your dreams. If you can manage this relationship then you can live a fuller life. The 7 Figures Plan is not about spending less money. It is more about working out your budget and how to apply your resources.

Going back to our boat, your expenditure adds weight to the craft. It makes the boat a more pleasurable place to be, but also slows down your progress towards your destination. You acquire more fancy stuff, but you also run the risk of forgetting to cover the basics in your vessel should a storm come your way. Don't forget that this added weight can mean you are forced to work harder on your manual labour. You may need to work harder just to keep the boat moving merely because your boat is getting overladen.

## Figure 5 - assets

Your assets are those items which can be used towards your future.

Assets give you freedom and choice. Your assets give you security so you have enough to cope with whatever life throws at you. Assets are what you can rely on to generate an income to fund the expenditure you want to live the life you desire in the future. In the 7 Figures Plan we will focus on building up the right kind of assets to give you the most flexibility to live the life you want.

Looking at your boat, your assets allow you to build a second propeller for your boat. This propeller is not powered by your hard work, but is powered by a different fuel. It works on its own to boost the forward momentum of your craft. This is achieved through income and capital growth generated by your assets. The additional power is slow at first, but gradually becomes so powerful that you can choose to stop working on the first propeller, if you want.

## Figure 6 - liabilities

Your liabilities are your debts. Liabilities are the opposite of your assets in that they are what hold back your future. Your liabilities take away from your security, although they can help you in some ways to achieve your shorter-term goals. In the longer-term they hold back your planning. Your liabilities are someone else's assets. Liabilities are an expenditure item, and as such hold back your income. In the 7 Figures Plan we will focus on reducing and eliminating your liabilities so that you can build up more assets.

Your liabilities are like added weight and corrosion, which drags on your boat. They add to your expenditure and hold back the forward momentum of the vessel. They also hold back the development of your second, automatic propeller. If not kept in check, this corrosion can bring your craft to a halt, or even make a hole below the water line.

## Figure 7 - protecting what you have

You should build up plans to protect what you have already accumulated and to preserve your current and future lifestyle. This means planning for potential pitfalls along the way, which includes disasters that could hold your ultimate goals back. Protecting what you have is a way to ensure security for your family now and in the future. It is less likely to allow you to live your dreams, but at least you will be able to maintain a decent lifestyle.

In some ways, protection is more important than the other 7 figures. However it is the last key figure since you need to know the other 6 figures to be able to calculate the $7^{th}$.

Your protection is like the safety features of your boat – GPS and lifeboats. These features cost you some money, but you'll be glad of them should a storm come your way. They'll prevent your boat from sinking, or at least get you to your destination should your boat sink.

### Other aspects

While I said that there are 7 Figures in your plan, we do need to introduce some other aspects from time to time. These will be included where they are important. They are typically less fundamental than the 7 key figures, but are important to examine.

Some areas are more advanced topics beyond the focus of this book. Where appropriate I flag these up for you so that if they are of interest you can seek out more information before making decisions. The goal of the 7 Figures Plan is to create a simple plan so you can take action. Some areas need more technical assistance but I want to give you the tools to take action.

## Timeline – putting it all together

I use the concept of a timeline to explain how to fit these aspects together. I find that using the visual aid is a neat way to put the figures together.

## *How does the timeline work?*

This is your life on paper. You were born on the left and you are travelling in one direction. We represent this on the timeline by placing a zero for your birth on the left of the scale. We assume you will live to age 100 on the right. Of course, you can change these figures to represent your own expectations but we generally assume you will live a long life. Why do this? The average life expectancy might be something like 86, but you might not be average! Therefore, it pays to err on the side of caution, or indeed positivity, since if you assume you will live to 86 and you actually live longer you will run into problems in your financial planning if you run out of cash.

We can use this timeline concept to map out what has gone in your life. We can also use it to visualise where your life is going, and how much time you have left to achieve your goals. Obviously, what has gone cannot be changed, so we can use the timeline to focus on what you can change, which is the future. Your actions from here drive your ability to achieve your future goals.

We do not use this to scare you or worry you. It is intended as a motivational tool to help you to realise that putting off action now will only make your job harder in the longer term. Time is your enemy in Financial Planning but it can also be your friend if you start taking action in small steps towards your goals.

The timeline will help you to put into focus what you want to do with the rest of your life, and how much time you have to achieve this. We will insert the various aspects of the 7 Figures Plan into the timeline, so you can bring it all together.

## Chapter summary

- You need to think into the future to make your financial plan work
- The 7 key figures you need to know are your age now, your goal age, your income, your expenditure, your assets, your liabilities and how much protection you need.

# Chapter 3 - Figure 1 – Your age

Your age is the first key figure in the 7 Figures Plan. No calculation is required. Your age now is important since this impacts your goals, desires, hopes and dreams. It also tells you something about your expectations for the future.

## Where have you come from?

### Skills and experience

You have a set of skills and experience that have got you successfully to this point in your life, and you can use these to help you to plan for the future. You need to be honest about your strengths and weaknesses in this area so you can aim to take rational decisions rather than emotional ones.

Most of what you need to learn in this book builds upon your existing set of skills. We all have the basic knowledge and common sense to apply these rules, but we just need to do them in a consistent manner.

My aim is get you to focus on the right skills and apply them to the most effect. You can then work out where you are lacking in skills and then either learn how to plug these gaps or hire the right person to do that for you.

### Financial elements

Depending on your background and your experience to date you will also have a set of financial resources (or liabilities) you can call on. Recognise that your past decisions and opportunities have got you to this point. Use this plan as a way to identify your financial positives and negatives. It is from this base that you can build some financial security, and then start to work on living your dreams. We will focus more on these areas in later figures.

### Build on the current situation

You should build on your current skills and financial assets, whatever they may be. Focus on the future from this point onwards so the only possible way is upwards. As you put in the hard work to analyse your situation and learn new skills you can only improve from where you are now.

## The past is gone

The past is gone and there is nothing that you can do about that. Recognise that your past experiences have got you to the point where you are now, whatever that means to you. If you can move your thinking towards the future you will have a much greater chance of achieving what you want from your finances.

## Don't dwell on your mistakes, learn from them

Of course you have made some mistakes with your financial planning in the past. We have all made significant errors in our Financial Planning. If you had not made any mistakes then you would not be human. Making mistakes and then learning from them is of key importance. Do not let your mistakes hold you back. Just make sure that once you recognise that you made a mistake that you do not let this paralyse you. Mistakes are a form of feedback and a primary way for us to learn. Every successful person in any field has had to make thousands of mistakes to be able to build a set of skills towards success. I can illustrate this with 2 examples:

## *Michael Jordan*

Michael Jordan was probably the greatest basketball player of his generation. He is famously quoted as saying:

"I've missed more than 9000 shots in my career. I've lost almost 300 games. 26 times, I've been trusted to take the game winning shot and missed. I've failed over and over and over again in my life. And that is why I succeed."

What does he mean by this? He knows the power of failure, because it is by failing that he learns how to succeed. He knows that by failing, by constantly practising and adjusting he can learn to become better. He was not born with the ability to make game winning shots. He became so skilled and reliable by constantly failing and practising every day.

You do not need to become the best in the world at Financial Planning. You just need to develop the skills you need to become better. Maybe that will prove to be enough for you. If it is not, then you can continue learning and developing your skills.

Recognise the mistakes you have made in your financial life. If you can do this you can put them aside so that you do not repeat them in the future.

## *Learning to walk*

You have seen children learning to walk. Are they all born with the ability to walk? No, of course not. But unless they have a physical reason to hold them back, the primal urge to get up and walk means that every child gets there eventually. We can learn a lot from this because each child learns through trial and error and by recognising their mistakes. No child gets it right the first time, but neither do they give up when they fail. They develop the will to want to stand; they practise the co-ordinated movements necessary; they develop the muscle strength. The list goes on. Each child will fail countless times before they master the technique. Of course, at this stage the child has not yet mastered more advanced techniques such as running, jumping and hopping.

We can easily apply this analogy to your own Financial Planning skills. You will certainly have some skills already. We will build on these rather than giving up when things do not go as you would want.

## Relating your age to your timeline

So how do we relate your age now to your timeline? Well, this is the easy part.

All you have to do is to place your current age relating to your position on the timeline. So in the example, below if you are 40 years old you would place a line on the timeline like so:

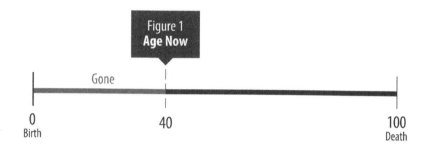

### What does this show you?

Your current age on the timeline is a way to focus you on what has gone in your life. This is not a negative, but is a simple fact. You can see how much time has been used to date, and how much time you might have left.

Focus on the time remaining to motivate yourself into action to change your future. You can not affect the past, but you can affect the future. Figure 1 should help you to gain some motivation for action.

## Chapter summary

- The past is gone, but has given you skills, experience and financial resources which you can use to build on
- Don't dwell on your financial mistakes, but learn from them
- Relate your current age to your timeline to give some context to what lies ahead

## Action plan

- Use the workbook at **7figuresplan.com/workbook**
- Answer the questions there as they will give you deeper insight into your past financial choices and experiences

# Chapter 4 - Figure 2 – Your goals

The second key figure in the 7 Figures Plan helps you to look into the future. If you want your future to be bigger than your past, you need to set a goal, and more specifically a goal age. Of course, you may have more than one goal. If this is the case you can take the 7 Figures Plan and adapt it so that you have a plan set up for each goal.

## Setting your vision - Start with the end in mind

This concept comes from the book *The 7 habits of highly effective people*, by Stephen Covey and takes us back to the concept of time travel. You must start living in the future to be successful in your Financial Planning. The alternative is to trust to luck, which is not much of a plan. If you start with the end in mind (your goal), you can then work backwards by using a Financial Planning to establish the steps necessary to take action to achieve that goal.

The best way to get what you really want is to build a vision of what you want to achieve. The more specific you can be the better. You need to almost be able to touch and feel the goal, so that you have a real vision of what you want. The more tangible it feels, the better the chance that you will work towards that vision.

You already have this skill and use it all the time. Let's use an example.

### Planning a journey – the right way

Every day you use this skill. Imagine you want to travel from London to

Edinburgh for a holiday. By examining a map you establish your current position, and are able to locate the place where you want to end up. You have many methods you can use to succeed in this goal, but the end point remains the same. By planning your final destination you will build a vision of what it is going to be like. You can consult travel brochures and websites. You can look up all the places to visit and hotels. These visual cues and recommendations will build up a picture in your mind based on your experiences and expectations so that you have an almost concrete vision of what the trip will be like.

Once you have an end goal in mind, you can then start narrowing down all the options so that you can choose the best for you. You may have a variety of factors to consider: perhaps cost, convenience and comfort. You have a variety of travel methods available to you: car, plane, bus, boat and train. The fact is that you are used to doing this kind of task, and are generally successful at doing it too. All you need to do is to apply the same skills to planning your financial future. I know it is more difficult, but it is much more worthwhile.

### Planning a journey – the wrong way

Consider the opposite approach, since this may also apply to how you currently approach your Financial Planning. This may also explain why you might not have been particularly successful in the past with your Financial Planning.

Imagine again that you want to travel from London for a holiday, but you have not taken the time to consider where you want to go. Suddenly the whole picture changes because the possibilities are endless. You wouldn't just set out on your journey hoping to end up at a wonderful destination, ready to enjoy your trip. You might end up at a great place, but how likely are you to succeed first time? This approach is extremely likely to fail.

How would you know what to pack? How much money would it cost? What method of transport would you use? In which direction would you travel?

The analogy works because you understand how to plan a journey, because you do it all the time. You just need to develop the same set of skills and apply it to an area which has a far greater scope for your lifestyle.

Imagine if you consistently apply the wrong methods to your Financial Planning. The results are far more likely to be worse than if you use the right methods. Over time these mistakes will only compound themselves so that you are far less likely to get to your ultimate destination.

### Changing the destination

You may wish to change your destination along the way. Once you get to Edinburgh it might not be the city for you (I have been there, and it is wonderful by the way!). Well, that is fine. You can just adjust your goals and expectations whenever you need to. You do not need to set your goals into concrete, but you do need to have something to aim at.

## If you don't set goals you can't measure success

If you set goals you can measure your success. This has a variety of benefits.

### Motivation

If you can see your progress, you can see how far you have come and how you are getting to where you want to be. This is a powerful motivating factor, and has the effect of speeding up your progress. One of the main reasons why people do not achieve their goals is not that they are too difficult. It is because they limit themselves – they give up. This is usually because they hit an obstacle along the way. Life is all about obstacles. You just need to recognise them as such, and work out a way to move around them. If you can focus on your long-term goals because they are set and established, you can then see the big picture and adjust your tactics to suit the situation.

Imagine you were on that journey from London to Edinburgh. You have chosen to drive there by car. Halfway there your car breaks down. Would you just give up on your goal? I doubt it because you would have a definite vision of what that means to you. If you had that vision from the outset you might have bought breakdown cover for your vehicle. This might then kick in to allow your car to be repaired by the roadside, allowing your journey to continue despite the temporary setback. This is a result of the logical side of you taking steps to plan for all eventualities and insuring against them, knowing the emotional impact of failure would have on your vision. Without that forward planning the emotional side of you might have taken over at this set back and sent you back to London.

Even if you have not considered the possibility of a breakdown to your vehicle, your vision of where you want to get to should still be strong enough to overcome the barrier in your way. If you want to get to Edinburgh strongly enough you would immediately change your tactics. You could easily switch your mode of transport from your car to a train. It might cost you more than you had planned before you started out, but you would end up in the same destination regardless of the pitfalls along the way. The power of having a vision of where you are going allows you to adjust to whatever life throws up in your way. You know these events will happen, so having the end in mind allows you to motivate yourself to overcome obstacles.

### Knowledge of what works (and what doesn't)

If you have an overall goal and vision of this goal you can start to measure your progress towards it. Again, our analogy of your trip works well. Your map tells you that the distance from London to Edinburgh is 332 miles, and you also know the direction of travel your need to take. You can therefore simply measure whether the actions you are taking are getting you closer to your goal or not. Armed with this knowledge you can review and adjust your strategy as you go so that you can stop taking actions which do not get you closer to your overall goal, and continue taking actions which do get you closer to your goal.

Your journey from London to Edinburgh will not go in a dead-straight line. The general direction of travel will be Northerly. However, you will need to travel in other directions from time to time as the situation demands it. You will constantly need to course-correct. The same happens with air travel. The general direction is set by the overall goal, but the pilot has to periodically adjust their course as they go.

If your car fails you, this does not necessarily mean that all cars will fail. You can use this knowledge to decide whether you need to switch your general mode of transport (say from car to train), or whether you just need to abandon one vehicle for another. You can apply this to Financial Planning. Just because your previous investments did not work out, does not mean that no investments can work out. It could be that you did not invest properly, or that something else went wrong.

### More likely to succeed

If you have a definite goal and a vision of that goal you are far more likely to succeed in getting to that goal. By having a target to aim at you are far more likely to hit it. You might not reach your goal, but you will give yourself a far greater chance of getting there if you focus first on what you want. Also, goals are not always absolute – they are not always all or nothing. You might have a goal of having a certain level of retirement income. If you miss that goal it would not be ideal, but taking some action towards that goal wold surely be better than no action at all. If 'failure' meant less than 100% then you would have still made some progress.

## How to set your goals and vision

It is difficult to translate the theory into practice in this area. You need to do a lot of soul searching to be able to really focus on what is important to you. This does not come easily, but the more you do it, the easier it becomes.

### *Work out what really motivates you*

You need to understand what really motivates you for this to be truly effective. This is very personal and can even be uncomfortable. The results can be amazing, and very liberating if you follow the process through. Try not to give up on this stage since it will have a powerful impact on later stages of the Financial Planning process. Think about your trip to Edinburgh. You might want to travel there to visit the city. What if you wanted to be there to watch a particular game of rugby? Surely your motivation would increase and would push you forward to achieve your goal.

The key here is to think big. Do not just focus on the easy goals or the traditional goals that society throws at you. You only get one crack at your life, so you owe it to yourself and your family to make the most of the time you have. The only limitations are set by yourself (within reason), so you have the opportunity to set goals as far reaching as you want. Just remember that the bigger the goal, the more work you will have to put in to achieve it.

Your goals do not have to be purely based on money. The money side affects every part of your life, and is really just the method that you can use to achieve what is really important to you. You can examine every aspect of your life:

- Money
- Family
- Other relationships
- Community
- Work
- Education and skills
- Travel and hobbies

The list is up to you.

## Why?

It is easy to understand the "What" and the "How" in our goals. But it is far more powerful to understand "Why" you want to do something. If you focus on that aspect you will have a far greater motivation, and the goal will resonate with you. Your "Why" is an emotional trigger, and the failure to achieve it could be painful. This should lead to a greater chance of success.

I recommend you read *Start With Why* by Simon Sinek. See **7figuresplan.com/resources**.

## George Kinder

George Kinder wrote one of the Financial Planning classics – *The 7 Stages of Money Maturity*. I recommend that you read it. The book will help you to establish what motivates you in your financial decisions, and more importantly why you take certain actions.

In particular the book has 3 key questions, which when answered in the correct order will help you to uncover what really motivates you. Once you have answered these questions you will have a great idea of your overall goals for your financial planning.

We list these 3 questions in our goal setting template. See **7figuresplan.com/workbook**.

When you start looking at goals your initial focus may be on material items. This is the easy area to quantify – your home, cars, holidays etc. When you start to consider your own mortality and limited funds you begin to focus on more fundamental areas like your family. You might love to have all the trappings of society but probably what really motivates you is relationships and spending time with those you love.

## The regrets of the dying

Some years ago I read an article (later turned into a book) by a former carer, Bronnie Ware (see **7figuresplan.com/resources**). She related the discussions she had held with many people in the last weeks of their

Dan Woodruff

lives. She explained the main regrets they had in the way they had lived their lives. This is a powerful reminder of what we value when we come to the end of our days.

## Not living your dreams

As soon as you lose your health this can be too late. Many people wish they had followed through on their dreams. If there is one message you should take from this book it should be that you have a responsibility to live your dreams, both for yourself and for those you love.

## Working too hard

Many wish they had not worked such long hours, and regret missing their children growing up. If you can establish what is important to you, you can make changes to your life. You might be able to put into context why you work so hard. Maybe you can cut back on what is unnecessary, or maybe you can focus on making the most of time outside of your work.

## Not expressing your feelings

his can be true of those who lose someone unexpectedly. Our lives are made meaningful by those who we love.

## Losing touch with friends and family

When it comes down to it, it is our relationships which define us, but this requires some work.

## Not being as happy as possible

It is easy to be negative and blame others, but it is your own responsibility to try to be as happy as you can.

## *Avoiding goal obsession*

This may be a strange point in a chapter about goals, but you should not let the overall goal mean you forget about living life on the way.

The key is to have some balance between living a good life now, while preparing for the future. It would not be right to work so hard to live a comfortable retirement, but not to see your family while you are pursuing this dream. Make sure you plan suitable small goals even while working towards to bigger goals.

## Bucket list

There was a film some years ago with Morgan Freeman and Jack Nicholson which explored the concept of a "bucket list". In the film one of the main characters is terminally ill. The 2 friends set out to achieve a list of accomplishments before he dies. The list was brought on by one friend seriously contemplating his demise. The film is actually a feel-good story, despite the negative backdrop. In the end, having achieved the items on the list takes second place to the relationship between the friends and the family members.

I have my own bucket list. On that list are a variety of things I would love to do before I die. Yours can be anything you want. On my list I have places to visit, skills to learn, items to own, events to witness. It was difficult to start the list, but once I got started I was able to quickly build up dozens of ideas. This helps you to think about the things you would love to do and experience and to bring them to life.

I do not look at the list very often, but when I do it surprises me. I find that I manage to knock items off the list without even realising it. It has a subconscious way of motivating me to try new things and reward myself for hard work on the way.

Of course, if I need inspiration for a reward or for the reason why I am working hard, I just need to look up the list. There is always an idea on that list to get me motivated to keep going.

The list is a great tool to review where I have come from. It is great to see the items get crossed off the list as I achieve them. This often happens without me realising it at the time. This review is a powerful thing since it makes me realise how far I have come on my life journey.

Once you start achieving items on your list you just start to work towards bigger and better goals.

# SMART goals

You may have already come across SMART goals. This is a neat way to set up your goals in the right way. If you follow this template you will have a much more concrete goal.

SMART stands for:

- **S**pecific
- **M**easurable
- **A**chievable
- **R**ealistic
- **T**imed

## Specific

If your goal is not specific enough it can be very difficult to track and to determine whether you are on target. The goal to be the richest man in the world is not specific enough. You need to be able to target your goal properly to have a chance of getting to it.

## Measurable

If you cannot measure your goal then how will you know if you are progressing towards it? If you measure your progress you will be able to say whether you have got there or not. This will be a motivating factor when you are partially there.

## Achievable

If your goal is too wild then honestly how likely are you to succeed? Let's face it, I would love to play professional sports, but at my age is this achievable unless I buy a team? Perhaps I need to adjust my expectations to something achievable for my skill and situation.

Realistic

You goal has to be based in reality. I would love to walk on the moon, but is this realistic? Maybe soon it will be. I would suggest that you are better off focussing on those areas where you have direct control.

Timed

Putting a time limit on your goal is extremely important. Otherwise the goal is open-ended and you can put off achieving it. If you put it off you are far less likely to get to where you want to be. The second of the key figures in the 7 Figures Plan aims to get you really focussed on the timing of your goals.

An example of a SMART goal

An example of a SMART goal might be to retire at age 65 with an income in today's terms of £20,000 per year. This is specific, measurable, achievable, realistic and timed.

## Prioritise

Once you have set your goals you may have too many to focus on for the moment. If you have more than 2 or 3 main goals this reduces the likelihood that you will achieve those goals. This is all down to focus. If you try to focus on too many things at once you will be pulled in many different directions. If you can focus on one or two goals at a time you can divert all your energy to a few tasks, and this will give a much greater likelihood of success.

You need to make notes of all your goals, and then work out which are the most important to you for the moment. Obviously, your life will change along with your priorities so you can always come back to these later.

By setting your top priorities you will gain the focus and clarity you need.

## Relating your goal age to your timeline

Relating your age to your timeline will help you to put your goals into context. In the previous chapter we focussed on your age now, and all the experiences which brought you to this point in your life. We now want to visualise how your goals relate to your current position.

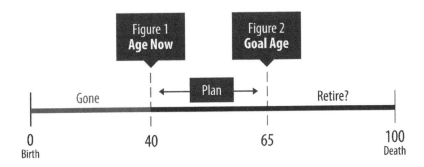

You should have already placed your current age on this chart in Chapter 3. Your own situation will look different to the example given. You need to place your goal age on the chart. Let's say you plan to retire at age 65. Put a second line on the chart at this point in your timeline.

### What does this show you?

This visualisation helps you to understand the size of the goal you have set yourself. This helps you to realise whether it appears to be realistic. In our example, your current age is 40 and you want to stop work at 65. This means that you need to accumulate enough assets in the following 25 years to fund your lifestyle for the following 35 years. Is this realistic? Perhaps it is, and perhaps it isn't. What this will probably tell you is that you are going to require some hard work and focus for the next 25 years. That's what this book and the 7 Figures Plan aims to help you with.

Your own situation will probably be different from the example shown. You might only have a few years between your current age and your goal age. In this case, the work required needs to be even more concentrated. You just need to be realistic and use your common sense to begin work in the right way.

# Advanced – assumptions and attitudes

As with many of the subjects covered in this book, there is always more to learn. This topic is related to your goal setting, but is not fundamental to the stripped down action plan which is the 7 Figures Plan.

These principles will allow you to create an even more accurate plan. If you want to keep things simple, just skip to the chapter summary.

## *What are assumptions and attitudes?*

To gain any degree of accuracy in your future planning you will need to make certain assumptions about how things may change. For example, we know that prices are likely to rise. Therefore, we cannot simply assume that the cost of living will stay the same. There are a variety of assumptions we can make about how things will change in the future, which allow your Financial Planning to be even more accurate. Your attitudes are also important since these determine your priorities in certain areas. If you are more concerned about certain areas, you will naturally elevate these in your priority list. If you are less concerned you might ignore these issues. This section aims to help you to decide which to focus on.

## *What would you gain from assessing your assumptions and attitudes?*

### Accuracy

Your assumptions allow you to estimate your goals with greater accuracy. If you ignore these issues you run the risk that you miss your goals because you underestimate the changes which occur over time.

Any changes you underestimate will have a more dramatic effect the longer the period between now and your goals. This could mean the difference between success and failure.

<u>Caution</u>

You should always be cautious since this means you are more likely to achieve your goals. If you make assumptions which are too optimistic you may miss these targets, and not hit your goals. Therefore, it pays to be cautious. If you do better than you had assumed, then you reach your goals quicker than you planned, which is great.

## Assumptions to consider

### *Inflation*

Inflation is the change in the cost of buying goods over time. Prices tend to rise over time. In certain categories this might not be the case, but as a general trend your expenses tend to rise.

Think about how much items cost 10 years ago. The price of a loaf of bread or a pint of milk was much lower than today. You need to factor this into your planning since if you ignore this change then you might not save enough to cope with the rise in the cost of living in the future. Imagine if you retire on a fixed income, but later find that you only have half as much money as you thought you would need to buy food. What would you give up?

In the UK, we have a number of measures of the rise in prices. The main ones are the Retail Price Index (RPI), and the Consumer Price Index (CPI). These inflation measures both take a list of items designed to approximate spending patterns and measures the change in prices over a given period. The Retail Price Index includes housing costs, such as mortgages and rents. The Consumer Price Index takes these out. The Consumer Price Index is the Government's preferred measure. It typically shows an inflation rate lower than the Retail Price Index.

Assumptions about inflation

The general trend has been for inflation to rise at about 3% per year over the last 10 years. Inflation is not a constant and there have been many periods when inflation has been higher or lower. You should take a realistic and cautious assessment of inflation, since it is the real killer of investment growth.

It could be argued that the costs of living for a retired person tend to rise quicker than for a working person. This is because retired people tend to spend more as a proportion of their income on higher inflation items such as food, fuel and heating. As a retired person your expenses could therefore rise at a much greater rate than the average person. You may wish to assume a higher factor for inflation as a result.

## Earnings and pensions

It makes sense for you to assess how your earnings will rise in the future. This will give you an indication of the likelihood that you will be able to put greater resources towards your Financial Planning as you keep your expenses under control. You can measure this through Average Weekly Earnings (AWE). The downside of this is that you are unlikely to be average. This measure will not take into account big changes in your circumstances, such as taking a career break, or getting a promotion. You will have to take a realistic guess.

You also need to take stock of how pensions are likely to rise in the future. Each pension scheme has its own rules on how benefits will rise in the future once they are in payment. Most company schemes rise in line with inflation. If you assume that inflation will rise at a greater rate than the rise in your pensions, then you need to bear in mind the gap in your planning.

State pensions currently rise at a different rate. There is the 'triple lock' which means that State pensions are likely to keep pace with the cost of living.

You decide on whether your Personal pensions should increase in value. You decide whether to take a higher initial pension income which never rises; alternatively, you can start with a reduced initial income but ensure that this keeps pace with the cost of living. All these issues need to be considered, especially if your main income comes from personal pensions.

## Expenses

You should assess your own expenses and work out whether each of them is likely to rise in the future, and at what rate. Each of your expenses may rise at different rates. You should consider how long they are likely to continue, and when they will stop.

For example, you might consider that your mortgage payments should have an end date, since you will repay the loan in time. If you fix the payments, you know that these will not rise with inflation and will stop at a certain point. After this end date you will have additional resources to allocate towards your longer-term goals.

Certain expenses, such as your heating bills, will always be present. You may decide that when you retire you will spend more time at home. Therefore, your heating bills might rise at that date

If you get this area right your Financial Planning will be more accurate. This will help you be more secure in you future. In practice, our professional Financial Planning focusses a lot on this area.

## Investment returns

Making assumptions about your investment returns is very important. Your investments such as your savings, pensions and property are likely to be the assets which you later rely on to fund your future lifestyle after you stop working. Therefore, the rate at which they grow will have a huge impact on the likelihood of reaching your goals, and the date at which you get there.

You should make assumptions about the rate at which your

investments are likely to grow, on average over time. Different types of investments are likely to grow at different rates, usually because of the risks you take. Cash investments will grow slowly, usually behind inflation. These generally serve a purpose towards short-term goals. More volatile investments such as shares and property are likely to grow at a greater rate over time, probably in excess of inflation. These should form the driving force behind your long-term planning.

### Charges

You should always be aware of the costs of your investments, since these will reduce the returns you make. It is probably easier to focus on the net returns after charges, and try to ensure that these generally beat inflation.

### Interest rates

Interest rates are important because they drive many areas of the economy. Low interest rates typically mean lower savings returns and lower borrowing costs. Obviously, this area is difficult to predict over any longer period.

### Tax

Tax is a cost you have to bear. You may want to give some thought as to whether your tax situation might change over your lifetime. For example, while you are working you might have less control over your tax affairs since your salary would be taxed at source. However, as your assets grow you may start to move into the realm of capital taxes. When you retire, your income tax rates might reduce if your income is lower. This can mean that your income requirements in retirement might be lower than in your working life.

## Attitudes to consider

### Investment risk

Your attitude towards investment risk is one of the most important areas of your Financial Planning. The choices you make could determine whether you are likely to reach your goals or to miss them. The risks you take with your money will influence the length of time you take to get to your goals.

<u>Risk vs returns</u>

In general terms, the greater risk you take with your money, the greater returns you should expect *on average over time*. "On average over time" is important here, because you should always expect fluctuations in the growth of your capital and income. The concept of investment risk is far beyond the scope of this book, and could be the subject of a book on its own. Here are some of the main issues for you to consider.

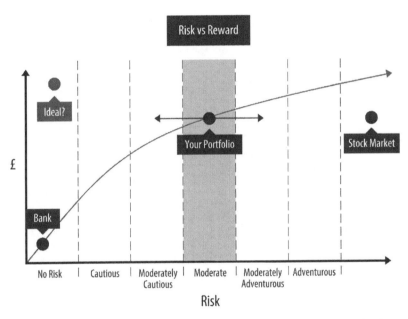

Those who take greater risks with their money tend to do better financially. Despite this, most people do not take risks with their money, and this can hold back their Financial Planning. I do not advocate that you take more risk with your money but you should understand the levels of risk that you are prepared to take, and work out what the expected returns are likely to be as a result.

There are two concepts at work here.

How much risk are you prepared to take?

How much risk you are prepared to take is like sticking a pin in your arm and working out the pain you can take before you say "ouch". This is the amount of risk you can bear before you find yourself waking up in the middle of the night worrying about the state of your investments.

How much risk do you *need* to take?

Actually, this is more important, but is often overlooked. For example, you might decide that you are a cautious investor. Let's say that a cautious investor could expect to achieve an example rate of return of 5% per year. If your Financial Planning showed that you needed to achieve a return of 8% per year, what does this tell you? This tells you that you need to take greater risks to achieve your goals at the date you planned. If you are not prepared to take greater risk then you need to adjust your goals. Perhaps you might accept a lower standard of living, or a later goal date.

The reverse might be true. If you are an adventurous investor you might expect that an example rate of investment return could be 9% per year. If your Financial Planning shows that you only need to achieve a 5% return to reach your goals then you might decide to take less risk, and therefore be more likely to reach your goals. My general philosophy is that if you do not need to take risk then you should avoid it. Of course, you may decide that you are prepared to take additional risk so that you get to your goals sooner, or to give yourself even better choices later.

Please bear in mind that these figures are not guaranteed, and are just given to illustrate an example.

## Capacity for loss

Capacity for loss assesses how much risk you are *prepared* to take, or the losses you can bear. Your attitude to risk is an intellectual exercise based in logic and experience. Your capacity for loss is an emotional response designed to keep you more cautious. This becomes more pronounced as you get older, and closer to your goal age.

Let's say that on paper you are an adventurous investor. Despite this, once you retire this is unlikely to remain the case. Since you are less likely to be able to earn that money again, your natural caution is likely to step in and get you to reduce the risks you take with your money. This is a good thing since it will enable you to hold on to what you already have.

You need to understand the relationship between your attitude towards investment risk and your capacity for bearing investment loss. If you find that suffering a short-term loss is likely to affect your Financial Planning you are likely to reduce the risks you take with your investments.

## Mortality

When you consider your future you must consider your inevitable death one day. This is not intended to depress you, but instead to motivate you to try to live the best life you can before your time runs out. The most precious resource we have is time, so we need to make the most of it. The timeline shows this in stark terms. We put your lifetime to age 100, but the reality is that the average person lives a shorter life. Of course, you might not be average, which is why we expand the period. After all, you would not want to reach the average date of death only to find that you have run out of money with many years ahead of you.

When considering your own mortality you can make certain judgements, which will affect your Financial Planning. For example, if your family is typically long-lived you might want to adjust your assumptions. If the reverse it true you might change your attitudes the other way. Just be cautious in this area.

If you have a medical condition this may affect your decisions. Consider yourself and your partner, plus what might happen to the survivor if one of you is not around.

## Morbidity

Morbidity is the likelihood of suffering serious long-term illness. Most of us do not think about this on a day to day basis. Despite this, you are probably well aware of people you know who have been affected by these issues. How did it affect their Financial Planning?

You attitude to the likelihood of you getting sick will impact the decisions you make with your Financial Planning. As medical science improves life expectancy, we have to face up to living with illness in later years for longer periods. This should be addressed in your Financial Planning.

We talk to many clients about the cost of inheritance tax. This tax is paid when people die and have assets over a certain value. Most people understandably want to avoid paying more tax than they should. However, what often happens is that their desire for security holds them back from doing anything about it. In many cases people think about the likelihood of getting seriously ill and needing long term care. We all know that nursing care costs a great deal. If you contemplate these issues, this might affect your Financial Planning and you might decide to hold on to assets rather than avoiding tax.

## Getting professional help

These are complex issues. You can probably see that while you can address them yourself, for each area you solve another takes its place. These are the kinds of issues that a professional Financial Planner will be well placed to help you to solve. If you find that you need to deal with some of the issues raised in this section, you might wish to consider engaging the services of a professional Financial Planner, who can focus on these technical areas on your behalf.

## Chapter summary

- Your goal age is very important to your Financial Plan
- Set your vision by starting with the end in mind
- If you don't set goals you cannot measure progress
- You make plans more than you realise – you just need to apply these skills to your finances
- Make your goals SMART and prioritise
- Relate your goals to your timeline to give you a sense of the size of the task ahead
- Think about the assumptions and attitudes that will guide your future action. How will these change and affect the plans you want to make?

## Action plan

- Use the workbook at **7figuresplan.com/workbook**
- Complete the timeline template to give yourself a visual representation of the work you have to do
- Think carefully about the future you want
- Complete your bucket list
- Set your short, medium and long-term goals
- Decide who you will use to keep you accountable
- Consider investment risks plus your attitudes and assumptions towards certain changes and risks

# Chapter 5 - Figures 3 & 4 – income & expenditure

Now that you have put to paper where you are and where you are going, we need to begin to put together the building blocks of your plan.

## 2 sides of the same coin

Fundamentally, what you earn determines what you spend. That's why we put income and expenditure together – they are 2 sides of the same coin. Obviously, if you do not have any income, it can be difficult to spend more. You should understand the relationship between your income and your expenditure, so you can examine your spending patterns. Some of your spending habits could be holding back your future Financial Planning. Your current self is spending the inheritance of your future self.

## The foundation of your Financial Planning

Your income versus your expenditure is the foundation of your Financial Planning. This is because your income and spending sits firmly within the gaps between your age now and your future goal age – figures 1 & 2 of the 7 Figures Plan.

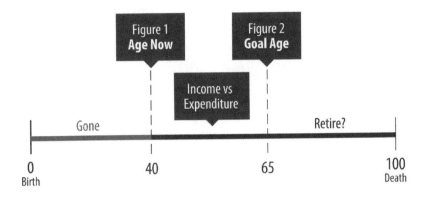

Without enough income you will not be able to live a decent lifestyle now. More importantly, without an excess of income you will not be able to put money aside to use in the future. The same goes for your spending patterns. If you spend too much now, you take money directly out of the pocket of your future self.

## Is your current self mortgaging your future self?

Are you driven by pressures put on you by society? You see the outward manifestations of wealth with your friends, family and colleagues. This is the outward façade we all put on our lives to show the best to the world. I get to see beneath the bonnet of many people's finances. I get to see them warts and all and often this is not pretty. I see many people who spend up to the limit (and more) of their earnings, regardless of whether they are low paid or high earners. This habit holds back their Financial Planning. In fact, it seems that it is often more difficult to live within your means when you earn *more* money. The pressures to spend and live the lifestyle of your peers are often so great that people spend far more than they need.

When you see all those shiny new cars remember that most of them are not owned by the person driving them. Most are either leased, are company cars, or are bought on credit. This *may* be decent tax planning, if you own a business. However, it is unlikely to be good

Financial Planning. The same goes for the big house, fancy holidays and other manifestations of wealth. For many people this often means mortgaging their future financial freedom in exchange for living for today. Of course, I am not saying that you should not do all of these things. The choice is yours. However, the choice may come down to whether you need to buy a new car every few years, or instead put that money towards a secure future.

Every time you spend money (outside of the necessities) you are making a decision. This decision is to enjoy your money now rather than to delay gratification in the future. Most likely these decisions are not thought through, and are probably driven by the emotional side of you. There are times when this is appropriate, but often we do not consider the implications of our actions (by listening to the logical side). I call this mortgaging your future. Most people think of a mortgage as a good thing – a way to buy a home. But a mortgage is a debt, which is taken on by your current self, to be repaid by your future self. When you buy a house your future self probably has to pay 3 times as much back in interest as your current self borrowed to buy the house. So, every time you spend money in the present, you take money away from your future self. If you have unlimited resources this is not a problem. Of course, if you are reading this book then I doubt this is the case.

You need to consider that if you spend money now you lose the ability to save that for your future, and therefore lose the investment growth on that money. Not only that, the cost of living, thanks to inflation, is likely to be greater in the future. The further away your goal age (Figure 2), the wider the gap is likely to be. Simple decisions made now by your emotional side rather than your logical side are likely to hurt your prosperity later on.

## Spend less than you earn – get rich slowly

This book is not about getting rich quickly. It is about using the resources you have now and in the future, and developing the habits to keep you on the path towards future security. If you follow these principles, you will develop and improve on good habits. You will take actions which add to your future security, not take away from it. If you follow these principles you will get rich, but it could take a long time. But you will be using time and compound interest as your friends.

## Live within your means

If you can live within your means you have a good foundation for your future Financial Planning. Financial maturity does not mean spending what you earn and no more. It certainly does not mean spending more than you earn. Financial maturity means spending less than you earn. It really does not matter what you earn (although it gets much more difficult if you earn minimum wage). What matters is how much you earn versus what you *decide* to spend. The gap between the two figures can be put towards your future. If you sleepwalk into letting emotional decisions guide you rather than logic you are likely to spend exactly what you earn now. Guess what? You'll be mortgaging your future.

### Case study - The high earning professionals

I remember seeing some new clients some years ago. Both were high earning professionals. One was on a six-figure salary, and the other was on his way. Outwardly, they had it all – the nice house, the cars, private school for the kids and holidays to exotic locations. But beneath the surface things were very different. They had zero control over their spending, and did everything on a whim. They would regularly overspend – so much so that they were actually massively in debt. They were influenced by other high earning professionals around them, who all exuded the outward trappings of wealth. Perhaps they were also on the path towards financial disaster too. This couple were approximately £100,000 in debt on credit cards and loans, over and above their mortgage. In the end I was not able to help them because they were not ready to change their spending habits. They had the means to get their finances back on track through fantastic income, but were unwilling to give up their spending. I am not in touch with them any longer, but I doubt their situation has changed.

Think about your own situation. Who is influencing your spending? Remember, spending is not bad, but *overspending* will have disastrous effects on your future self.

### Put the rest towards your future

If you can spend less than you earn you can use the difference to put towards your future. You will switch from mortgaging your future to building a nest-egg for your future. The greater the gap between your income and expenditure, the more you can put aside.

You may feel that you can not put much aside at present. The most important thing to do is to start, however small. Saving money is a habit. This is a habit which needs to be nurtured so that the bad habit of overspending does not come along to undo all your hard work. If you analyse your spending patterns you can find ways to improve the gap between your income and expenditure. This will help you to get your spending under control (if needed), and then you can start to put more towards your savings for the future.

### Understanding your decisions

Remember, spending is necessary. Just make sure that you understand the reasons and motivations behind your spending patterns. You do not have to stop spending on the nice things in life. After all, I have already told you a story of how life can be short. It would be a pity to save your money for a rainy day but never get to enjoy it. What I am advocating is some sort of balance, and particularly so you can avoid overspending.

So, think less about cutting back. Think more about understanding the ramifications of the decisions you make. If you can introduce some control over your spending you will start to see some real progress in your overall wealth.

## Tax is an expense

When I ask most people what they earn, they can easily tell me. What they usually tell me is their income before tax (gross income). This is how income is usually presented. You should think of tax as an expense you have to bear. This will radically change your thinking on the income you need, and the effect of your spending.

<u>An example</u>

Let's say you earn £30,000 per year. You therefore earn £2,500 per month. If you are an employee, income tax and National Insurance (another tax) will be deducted by your employer and paid to the Government. At the time of writing, this would leave you with a net income of £23,218. This represents tax of 23% of your earnings.

What you should really focus on is your take-home salary – the net position after tax. Instead of £2,500 per month, you actually earn £1,934, which is quite a different position. Remember, this is just an example, and your situation will be different. But the principle is the same – tax is an expense.

Let me put this into context. Let's say you want to buy the latest shiny gadget. I'll leave you to decide if this is spending or overspending! The shiny gadget costs £500. That represents 20% of one month's salary using the example above. But if we realise that tax is an expense, you actually need to earn £649 to get a net income of £500. Suddenly you start to see your spending in a different light. If you use credit to buy that item, the costs start to go through the roof.

Remember, that income taxes are not the only impact on your spending. There are dozens of taxes in the UK, and they affect us all differently. I understand and support the fact that we need taxes to fund our country – after all, we need roads, hospitals and schools.

## Borrowing

Borrowing seems to be part of our way of life. Just remember that borrowing to spend today means mortgaging your future self. Every £1 you borrow now means interest payments which have to be met by your future self.

An example

Let's go back to our example, where you earn £30,000 per year and your net income after tax is £23,218. You still want to buy that shiny new gadget. You've done your homework and shopped around for the best deal. The retailer has a special offer and is providing you with a free carry case for your item. The problem is that you do not have the spare cash this month to afford it. "Don't worry," says the salesman, "you can have it on a monthly payment plan." You can pay over 48 months (4 years), and the interest rate is "only" 30%. The cost to you would be a mere £18.20 per month. "To get a £500 item, with the latest, shiny gizmos? What a bargain, I'll take it!" you say.

After the paperwork is completed, you'll notice that the total to pay is not £500; it's now £855. You pay £355 over the odds for the item (mortgaging your future self, who won't have this money to spend later, and after the gizmo is obsolete).

But it gets worse. Remember we said we needed £649 earnings before tax to buy an item for £500? Now you are not buying an item for £500, you are buying it for £855. That means that to have that money in your pocket after income tax you need a salary of £1,100. This is really starting to hurt. Your £500 purchase actually cost you over double the price you thought you were paying – 120% more in fact. But at least you got a free carry case!

This example above might seem a little extreme, but it does happen all the time, and in many cases can be worse. Think about payday lenders with exorbitant rates of interest, many of which can be over 1000%. When you take the time to consider your purchase decisions you may begin to think again whether you need items or whether you can wait, perhaps until you have saved enough money to buy the item outright.

Using credit to fund lifestyle spending is one of the worst things you can do to your future self. You are simply taking money out of your future pocket to buy items which would have no benefit to your future security.

We will explore credit and debt in Chapter 6.

## Expenditure analysis

An expenditure analysis will help you to understand where all the money goes. From this you will be able to start to work out how you make financial decisions. You can probably group certain items together, and possibly make improvements in your spending.

Having this knowledge means that you can start to understand how your lifestyle works. As a result you will be able to take action to make improvements. You can work out what is strictly necessary, and what you could do without if you are motivated to make a change for the future. This will be very personal to you.

## What to track?

There are many ways that you can track your expenditure. It just takes a workable method and some common sense. Below, I have set out how I do it. I have also incorporated this into my income versus expenditure template (see **7figuresplan.com/workbook**). This template gives you a basic framework for you to put in all the items of expenditure.

I encourage you to track everything you spend. You could keep a journal, or all your receipts. I use an app on my smart phone, and track all the spending I make, along with my wife. When you analyse this data you get a great understanding of where the money goes. Actually, just having to write it all down can sometimes act as a brake on unnecessary spending.

### Be honest with yourself!

Tracking your spending habits is not easy. You need to be honest with yourself. You can easily sweep certain spending under the carpet, perhaps because you spent cash, or because it is only spent once a year.

This is dangerous because if you ignore some items, you will not have a full picture. It is easy to fool yourself that you have more left over than you really have. I see this all the time, especially in certain spending areas. This is particularly true of discretionary spending like entertainment, and things like holidays. I remember talking to one client who told me that he spent £2,000 a year on hobbies and holidays. When I quizzed him about his recent trip with the family to Disney World in Florida (with 3 kids), plus the expenses of his glider, the position changed to something nearer £10,000. He was not deliberately misleading himself, but you can easily see how an £8,000 difference in his spending would impact on his plans.

## Committed expenditure

We run a simple spreadsheet with all our committed expenditure in it. This is broken down by month but covers a whole year, a bit like how a business does a cashflow forecast. What this does is to try to cover all the items which go out immediately each month – the council tax, utilities, insurances and the like. We also include committed savings and payments towards other pots of money like tax or holidays. Looking at the data over a year means that we cannot ignore certain irregular committed expenses such as our car insurance which is paid annually rather than monthly.

On this sheet, we also put our regular monthly income (after tax). This gives us a neat outline of how much is coming in each month, and how much we expect to go out each month. As your bills or income change you can always update the figures. The point is to cover all the predicable spending here.

At the bottom of the sheet we have some money left over. This is used to fund our discretionary budgets. See below.

### Separate pots – pay yourself first

We build up separate pots of money to be used towards specific projects. This might include building up savings, paying a tax bill, or building up a holiday fund. The pots should make sense to you, but the money that goes into each pot is taken from our monthly committed expenditure.

The idea is that you should pay yourself first. If you can automate the process of saving towards other pots of money, then this will become a habit that you do not have to think about. If a certain amount goes into a separate account each month to be used towards your holiday then it will just happen unless you intervene for some reason. This works well when you pay your mortgage, which benefits your lender, so why shouldn't it happen in your favour when you save towards your goals?

## Variable expenditure

This will be different for you. You might not want to track spending in exactly the same way that we do it. But you should do something like this. Create a system which works and makes sense for you. You might not agree with the categories we use, so simply change them to adjust to how you run your life.

We track 2 separate areas. Firstly, we keep all our receipts. Every time I use my payment card I get a receipt, and keep it in my wallet. If I withdraw cash, I get a receipt as well. My wife does the same. If we did not do this, it would be easy to overlook where the money went.

### Food

We have 2 discretionary budgets: for food spending and other discretionary spending. Food spending is self-explanatory – that is anything spent in the supermarket or on lunches and the like. The reason that we include this in our variable spending is that we find that this is not predictable. We can go for some weeks spending lower amounts, but in others we need more expensive items. Most people underestimate how much they spend on food (by around a half). This is because they usually only consider what they spend at the supermarket on their weekly shopping. They forget about the takeaways, the newspapers, the lunches and other top-ups. By tracking everything, we know what we really spend.

We have a monthly budget for food, contained within our committed expenditure spreadsheet. We then keep a log using an app on our smart phones, which shares the data. Each item of spending is logged in the app, and we track the remaining amount for the month. This allows us to know if we are getting close to the limit. You can do this with a simple log sheet, which you total as you go along, or at the end of the month.

Discretionary spending

We also have a budget for discretionary spending. This can be anything else which does not fit into any other category. It also includes unexpected items, which crop up from time to time. If I want to buy myself an item of clothing, it goes on this list. If I spend money on a night out it goes on this list. The point is that we have a budget or an allowance for discretionary spending, and we do not feel bad about spending it. The money is there to be spent. However, we do have a limit on that spending. If we reach that limit then something has to give.

## Stop when you reach limits

The reason that we laboriously track all this spending is so we can build up a pattern over time. Sometimes we overspend, and we analyse the figures to work out behaviours which might need to be altered. Alternatively, the cost of living might be going up, as it tends to do, so we might need to reduce spending elsewhere, or increase our income.

When you get to the limit of spending in a discretionary category then you need to do one of two things. Either you need to stop spending, or you need to bring in money from elsewhere. To give an example, let's say our food budget is £500 and our discretionary spending budget is £500 as well. If our discretionary spending reaches the limit we will either need to stop spending until the next month, or to take this money from another sources. This could be from our food pot, or from savings. If there is not another pot of money, then stopping should be the only option – certainly not using credit since that is mortgaging your future.

This exercise develops discipline in your spending habits. If you reach a limit you should stop spending. If you are not prepared to stop then at least if you force yourself to take the money from another source you might take a moment to think about the implications of reducing that pot. Taking money out of your holiday fund might mean a less exciting trip next year.

### Save the remainder

As you develop discipline in your finances you may spend less. You can create items of savings in your committed expenditure. But you might be able to underspend in your discretionary spending as well. If this is the case, you can move this money at the end of the month into another pot like your savings or holiday fund. Over time this becomes quite motivational as you can see the effect of your spending discipline as how this is helping you to get closer to your other goals.

## Figure 3 – your annual income before tax

Figure 3 in your 7 Figures Plan is your annual income *before* tax.

This can come from a number of sources:

- Salary
- Bonus
- Overtime
- Commission
- Dividends
- Business profits
- Interest
- Investments

Our income vs expenditure worksheet will help you to break this down and to calculate Figure 3. See **7figuresplan.com/workbook**.

## Figure 4 – your annual expenditure

You should calculate your annual expenditure, and the income vs expenditure worksheet will help you to do this. We break this down into categories such as:

- Annual committed household expenditure
- Annual discretionary expenditure
- Money being put towards your goals
- Tax

## Using figures 3 & 4

We are interested in the difference between figures 3 & 4. The difference (if positive) can be put towards your future goals, which is the whole point of this chapter.

## Income & expenditure on the timeline

Let's examine the effect of all this on your longer term plan and relate it to your timeline.

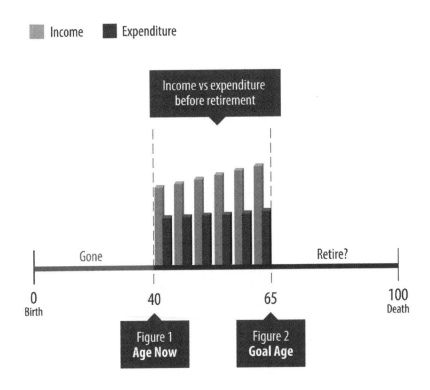

Once you know the figures for your income and expenditure you can plot them on your timeline for the current year. You can then start to think about how this might change in years to come, using some of the assumptions you made in Chapter 4. If you plot these assumptions on to the timeline it will help you to come up with some visual clarity around how the figures interact now and in the future. Over time, you would hope that your income would improve, while your expenses do not increase too much. If this is the case then the increasing difference can be used towards your future.

Later on you can assess the possible income sources for your goal age, making realistic assumptions about how the assets you generate are able to produce an income to pay for the inevitable expenses.

This might look something like this.

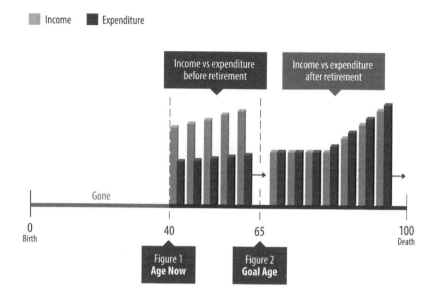

## Chapter summary

- Your income and your expenditure are the primary drivers of your current and future lifestyle
- Income and expenditure are both sides of the same coin, and cannot exist apart
- Think about your current self vs your future self –are your current actions mortgaging your future self?
- A general principle is that you should spend less than you earn and put the excess towards your future
- Tax is an expense, so make sure you understand its effects
- Borrowing to spend on your lifestyle should be avoided
- Understand your income and how this is taxed
- Analyse your expenditure to bring some discipline to your finances
- Establish how much excess you have (if any)

## Action plan

- Use the workbook at **7figuresplan.com/workbook**
- Complete the Income vs expenditure template provided.

This will help you to understand the sources of your income, and how this might be improved. You will also be able to analyse your spending patterns to see whether you can make changes for the better.

# Chapter 6 - Figures 5 & 6 – Assets and liabilities

Just as your income is linked to your expenditure in your financial planning, so are your assets and your liabilities. Think of the difference between your income and expenditure as the engine room of your financial plan. Your assets and liabilities are the foundation on which you can build your future security and lifestyle. You can only get to financial security and freedom by having assets. Your liabilities will hold back your ability to accumulate assets.

## What are assets and liabilities?

Your assets are anything that you can rely on in your future to generate more capital and income. Your assets are the building blocks of your future self's ability to become financially secure and financially independent. You probably have assets already: property, investments and pension funds. You just need to build enough assets to be able to securely pay for your future self's expenses.

Your liabilities are your debts. Liabilities are not your expenses (we covered expenses in the previous chapter). There is some overlap given that the cost of your liabilities becomes an expense in your budget. Since your debts cost you money, they will hold back your ability to generate assets. Most people of working age have some form of debt: mortgages, loans and credit cards.

## 2 sides of the same coin

Your assets and your liabilities are 2 sides of the same coin. In general,

Dan Woodruff

your assets work in your favour and your liabilities work in someone else's favour.

## Assets work in your favour

This is vitally important. Your assets are the foundation on which you will build a secure future for yourself. Assets, particularly *good assets* (see below), enable you to generate an <u>income</u>. You may also have some flexibility to use these assets when you need them.

It is vital to focus on this income. You currently have your income from your job or business. But you have to work to get this income. Your most precious commodity is your time, since you know this is a dwindling resource. Therefore you should aim to replace the income from your work with an income from another source. The sure way to be able to do this is to generate enough assets to be able to provide enough income to live the life your future self wants.

You probably need to generate significantly more in assets than you might have thought. It depends on your goals, which is why it is important to put them into context using the 7 Figures Plan.

## Liabilities work in someone else's favour

Your liabilities or debts are someone else's assets. Therefore, if you borrow any money you make someone else richer, and yourself poorer. This is the power of interest. Debt is a significant cost, often for many years. This expense directly removes cash from your budget, and stops you from accumulating further assets, which could have been used to make you financially free. This is why your assets and liabilities are 2 sides of the same coin –they have a direct influence on each other. Your goal should be to become debt free as soon as you can.

When you take out a loan with your bank this becomes an asset of the bank. That is because your loan and liability becomes a source of income for the bank for many years. The loan can even be sold on to another institution. The question is whether you want to be building assets for yourself or someone else?

# The power of compound interest

Albert Einstein famously said that compound interest is "the most powerful force in the universe." This is because it is so subtle, but builds up so powerfully over time. It is so subtle that it is easy to underestimate it. Compound interest can work in your favour, or for someone else's benefit; it can build your future or take away from it.

Compound interest is the effect of earning interest on top of interest. This has a powerful cumulative effect over time. The trouble is that human beings tend to think in a linear way, and that's not how compound interest works.

Example

Let's say you saved £1000 in a bank account which paid you 10% interest. This is not a realistic example at the time of writing, but the figures have been chosen to make the calculations easy to follow.

| Year | Balance | Interest | Total |
|------|---------|----------|-------|
| 1 | £100 | £10 | £110 |
| 2 | £110 | £11 | £121 |
| 3 | £121 | £12.10 | £133.10 |
| 4 | £133.10 | £13.31 | £146.41 |
| 5 | £146.41 | £14.64 | £161.05 |

Dan Woodruff

Let's look at this as a chart over a longer period.

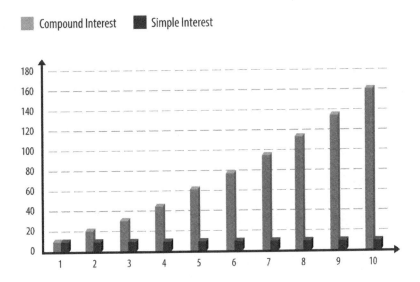

This shows the power of compound interest. The chart does not grow in a straight line as you might expect with a simple interest calculation. The balance grows exponentially. Why is this?

The interest earned in year 1 is added to the balance. Each year, interest is earned on the initial sum, as well as the interest. Therefore, the interest earned for each year earns interest. Over time this builds up into a powerful force.

This is why we encourage you to start saving now, no matter how small the amount may be. Over time, you would be amazed at how the relatively small amounts can build up into something huge. You should also be careful to find out whether your bank pays you interest on a simple basis or a compound basis.

The power of compound interest can also work against you in the form of liabilities. Debts usually charge higher interest rates than you get for your savings. Therefore, the effect of compound interest on your liabilities can be much bigger, and work against you in a debilitating way. This is why it is usually sensible to pay off debt before you save.

# Types of assets

There is not a best type of asset, but they each have different characteristics, so you need to consider these before you commit your excess income.

## *Pots for different needs or goals*

If you start to think of your individual goals, you might want to create different pots for each goal, depending on your needs. With a short-term goal like buying a car you might want to save in a secure asset which has instant access. If your goal is longer-term like retirement, you might consider that you want the assets to grow (using compound interest), and so might not need instant access.

## *Cash*

Cash tends to be the most secure form of asset and is usually the easiest to access. You might know cash accounts as your standard bank savings accounts. They tend to be safe since the capital does not grow but pay a pretty poor rate of return, often behind inflation. For this reason, you might want to use these accounts for your day to day expenses, and other short-term goals like saving for a holiday or paying your tax bill.

Since bank accounts tend to pay rate behind inflation, you are likely to lose money in the longer-term if you have too much money in your bank account.

If you want to avoid risk completely, then a bank account is probably right for you.

## *Property*

Property is your house and other property which you might rent out for a profit. Property tends to be quite secure in the longer term, but there can be wild fluctuations in valuations of these assets due to demand issues and the cost of credit. In general you should not think of property as a short-term investment. Typically you would expect that your property would do well in the long term.

Because of the nature of property, it can take a while to release funds held, and there are additional taxes to consider.

## Investments

Investments come in the form of a wide variety of different tax wrappers. In general, investing money can generate much greater returns over time than property or cash. This can come with greater risk, although it does not have to. Many investments pay both an income and allow the capital to grow. This can have a powerful influence on the growth of the assets over longer periods. The downside is that you must be prepared to see some fluctuation in the value of your assets both upwards and downwards.

In general, investments are more flexible since you can access the money whenever you want. They can also be more tax-efficient.

## Retirement funds

Retirement funds are a great way to build tax efficient savings for you over the long term. The downside is that there are significant restrictions on what you can and cannot do with your money. You would probably find the tax efficiency of pension plans to be attractive, but the payoff for this is that you cannot access this money until later in life, and must then use the funds to purchase an income which is taxable. Recent changes to retirement accounts mean they are far more flexible than in the past.

## Businesses

Businesses are a form of asset which can generate significant returns, often at much higher returns than with other assets. Of course, this tends to be because greater risk has been taken so you need to be careful about how you invest in a business.

### Other

Other assets might also form part of your plan for the future. You could own more esoteric assets like antiques, wine or stamps. These have a tradable value, but not in the way that a more mainstream investment might work. Therefore, they can be much more volatile in their valuations.

Other assets do not grow in a way that is useful to you. Think of your car as an example. Unless you have a classic vehicle, it is likely that your car is a depreciating asset. This means that it is losing money each year.

## Good assets vs bad assets

In financial planning there are good assets and bad assets. If I was to ask you the question 'What is your most valuable asset?' what would be your answer? I bet that you probably answered that it is your house. This is *not* an asset in financial planning terms. In fact your house is one of your biggest liabilities.

You have been told that renting is dead money and you save money in the long term by buying a house. I cannot argue with this sentiment because you need somewhere to live. Unless you plan to downsize at some point, you are unlikely to be able to realise the capital stored in your house. Your family will access this when you die, but you probably won't get to see it. If you sell your house you need to buy another one.

There is nothing wrong with buying a property to live in. You just need to recognise that this is a purchase that will not help you with your Financial Planning goals. What is more, your property is likely to be one of your biggest liabilities. You must pay for a mortgage (a liability). You must also pay many expenses associated with owning a property – utilities, maintenance, local taxes. Hopefully, you are seeing your property in a different light now. Your house is a *bad asset*.

So what are *good assets*? A good asset is anything which is readily realisable and income producing. You can sell readily realisable assets at any point and spend the proceeds on your lifestyle. Assets that are income producing tend to grow over time using compound interest. You can see that your house does not fall into this category.

Good assets are assets like bank accounts, shares, investment accounts, ISAs. You could make a case for rental property, although they tend not to be instantly accessible, since property can take a long time to sell.

Pension plans are not good assets in this sense since you have restrictions from the Government on what you can and cannot do with your money. This does not mean that you should avoid pensions, but it does mean that you should recognise their limitations and look to build up some more flexible good assets alongside your pension plans.

Take a moment to divide your assets into good assets and bad assets.

## Emergency fund

An emergency fund is a pot of money that you can use to pay for an unexpected bill or short-term disaster.

### Why have an emergency fund

An emergency fund is there to stop you from cashing in your longer term assets should you need cash in a hurry. It should also mean that you avoid using expensive credit when you need money. Both of these scenarios are bad for your long term Financial Planning since they would hold back your future financial security.

Imagine you come home from work one day to find that your boiler has broken down and you will need to spend £1,500 on a replacement. You could dip into your ISA fund to pay for this, or you could borrow on your credit card to pay the bill. Neither option would be good. If you cash in some of your longer term savings this might come with some transaction fees. It might coincide with a dip in the stock market, and might not be the right time to sell. By taking money out of this fund you are losing compound interest that your future self might have used to generate financial security.

Borrowing money would be even worse. The borrowed money would attract interest, probably at a high rate. This would immediately put up the cost of the replacement boiler by a significant amount since the capital and interest would need to repaid over time. Your £1,500 emergency purchase might end up costing you £2,500.

The better alternative is to have an instant access bank account with enough money put aside to make you comfortable that you could cover any short-term unexpected expenses. This prevents you from dipping into your longer term savings, or using credit to cover short-term emergencies.

Your emergency fund should be separate to other short-term savings pots. Your emergency fund is not your tax fund and it is not your holiday fund. If you combine these funds, you run the risk of depleting these pots of money just when you might need them. What would happen if your boiler broke down just before your tax bill became due?

## How much?

How much you should have in your emergency fund depends on your personal situation and how comfortable you want to feel. You should have enough to cover short-term emergencies, but not any more than this. You want to put any excess to work for you. It is unlikely that bank accounts would provide you with enough growth over the long term. I recommend that you put aside 3-6 months worth of household expenditure in an instant access bank account. Add to this any other funds you might need for planned projects like buying a car or taking a holiday. If you are risk averse put aside more. For example, if you are self-employed you might recognise that you can have periods where your income is limited. Therefore, you might want to build up a bigger emergency fund.

Take a look at your instant access accounts. Do you have too much or too little in your emergency funds?

## Advanced – investment theory

This book is not about investing your money. This subject is huge and could be the subject of a book in its own right. However, it makes sense to consider the issue alongside your assets, since you are going to save money towards your future at some point. When this happens, you are going to need to consider investing some of this money.

### *Why consider investing money?*

If you save money in a bank account you get a relatively low rate of return on your money. Usually, this return is behind inflation, which means that you will lose money in real terms over the long term. Therefore, if you need your money to grow faster than inflation you should consider taking additional risk so that your money works in your favour. This can generate additional growth on your assets, which helps you to get to your goals faster. Of course, with investments comes additional risk, so this section is designed to help you to get some understanding of how risk works.

You have probably invested money in the past, perhaps without really considering it. Most of us invest money through our pension schemes, even if this money is placed into a default investment fund. This plan invests money on your behalf, and this will grow or lose money as a result of your decisions.

### *What do you want from your investments?*

This depends on a number of factors, such as your financial stability, your age and what the money is to be used for. You should think clearly about your strategy for your investments and what the end point should be. Think about the following issues:

1. Do you need to grow the money?
   This applies to you if you want to build a pot towards a future

goal, such as retirement or the purchase of a house. If the money is for a short-term project this is less of an issue.

2. Do you need income from this money?
   This applies to you if you need to add to your income from other sources – perhaps you are retired or are taking a break from working. If you do not require an income, you should be looking to grow the money to make the most of it in the future.

3. When will you start to spend the money, and for how long?
   You should think about this issue even if you don't have a need for the money right now. Otherwise, you might never make use of it, which means you lose the ability to make your own or someone else's lifestyle more comfortable.

4. How experienced are you with investing money?
   Many amateur investors make costly investment mistakes that an experienced investor would not make. Be honest with yourself on this issue.

5. How well do you understand investing?
   Never invest in something you cannot explain to someone else. If it is too complex then the chances are it is probably not for you. Most investment decisions should be logical and straightforward unless there is a very good reason to do otherwise. Commit yourself to education to help you to make informed decisions. Equally, you might decide to outsource investment decisions to a professional. It helps to have some understanding since this can allow you to choose the right investment professional for you.

6. How much risk are you prepared to take to get to your goals?
   You should never take more risk than you feel comfortable with, but we often find that people either take too much or too little risk with their money.

7. How much can you afford to save now and in the future?
   The 7 Figures Plan should help you to work out the answer to this question. Think about how much you are prepared to invest in your future lifestyle.

## Understanding your investments

It is your responsibility to get enough education to understand your investments, *even if* you take advice from an adviser. You can access useful information from websites, newsletters, blogs and the financial press. A good starting point is to get a quality broadsheet newspaper at the weekend, as these usually have a good money section.

If you do not understand a product or the reasons for it, then you should not invest in it. You should keep things as simple as possible without good reason. Most complex financial products are created to help the adviser to make a sale rather than to look after your interests. Therefore, if you educate yourself in the investment process you will help yourself to avoid costly mistakes later on.

## Take emotion out of investment decisions

Most people do not take investment decisions in a strategic fashion. Think about all the influences you may have on how and where to invest – your family, friends, colleagues, the bank, financial advisers etc. Few of these have a financial stake in the outcome of your decisions no matter how sure they are of their advice.

Look at investment fundamentals and try to take the emotion out of your decisions. Over time certain actions will yield results no matter what the prevailing economic conditions. Investment bubbles come and go, but the general trend is upwards, and if you follow the processes in this section you should generally come out on top.

Without a considered and repeatable investment process you will not be able to get the best out of your investments. Many investors fail because they do not apply a consistent approach to their investing. Take a step back and analyse the best way forward and you should avoid costly errors.

## How much risk or security do you need?

Investment management is designed to manage risk. All investments involve some sort of risk, from almost no risk, to a high level of risk. In general terms it can be said that the greater the risk you take the greater returns you should generate on average over time; the reverse is also true.

Therefore, over time you should expect low risk and low returns on assets such as cash or bank accounts (perhaps below inflation), and greater risk and greater returns on riskier assets such as shares.

Examining risk vs return

The chart below shows a theoretical measure of the ideal relationship between risk (along the bottom axis) and returns (along the left axis). As the risks taken increase, so do the returns over time, although greater volatility comes with this.

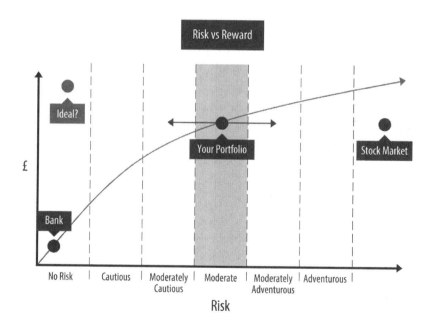

A low risk asset such as a bank account sits in the bottom-left corner of the chart – low risk with low returns. Riskier assets such as shares move towards the top-right of the picture.

In theory, the "ideal" investment sits at the top-left of the chart. This represents low risk with high return. Have you ever been promised an investment product like this? Has it ever delivered? In my experience, most of these schemes are scams, or are hiding the real risks of the investment. They may appear to be low risk, but in fact take much greater risks with your money.

Decide how much risk you are prepared to take, and then understand what the likely returns should be over time for this level of risk. This will give you something to use to predict your investment returns. Your investment planning should then be about keeping you within this level of risk, as demonstrated by the shaded band in the chart above.

## How much risk are you currently taking

Most people do not stop to think about how much risk they are taking with their investments. Risk varies between investment types, but this is a broad guide to what you should expect from investments:

| Asset | Risk level | Example |
|---|---|---|
| Cash | Low | Bank accounts; cash ISAs |
| National savings | Low | Premium bonds |
| Government bonds | Low to medium | Gilts |
| Corporate bonds | Low to medium | Corporate debt |
| Property | Medium | Houses |
| Managed funds | Medium to high | Pension & investment funds |
| With profits funds | Low to high | Pension & investment funds |
| Shares | High | Shares & investment funds |

Take the time to evaluate the level of risk you are currently taking - it may surprise you. This can be quite difficult to get right without some professional advice, since some investment providers are quite good at clouding the issue of risk. They use all sorts of sexy-sounding names for their investments, but you must look underneath the bonnet a little to understand what is actually happening.

You may be surprised by just how much risk you are taking. We see elderly people taking massive risk, and younger people taking almost no risk. If you can understand where you are now, and compare this to where you need to be to get the returns you desire, you have a better chance of reaching your longer term goals.

## How much security do you need?

How much risk you can bear before you wake up at night worrying about your decisions. Your risk appetite is shaped by your investment experience and expertise. Once you know this, you are in a better position to help you to choose investments which do not take too much risk.

You may need more security with some of your goals. If you plan to make a big purchase in the next few years, you might want to consider keeping some of your money in cash so that it will not drop in value and be easy to access. For other goals you might be prepared to take greater risks. For example, you might want to take more risk with your long-term retirement pot.

## How much risk you need to take

This is an important distinction, since you might place your tolerance for risk differently to what you actually *need to take* to achieve your goals. If you describe your risk profile as moderate, but you only need to take cautious risks to achieve your goals, then why take the extra risk? If you do not need to take risk, then why do it? The reverse is also true – some cautious investors should consider taking extra risks to achieve their goals. If you are only prepared to take low risks but your plan shows that this will not get you to where you want to be by the date you have set, then you need to make some change to your plans. Either you will need to adjust your expectations or take additional risk.

## How risk works in practice

How likely are you to lose money if you invest in the UK stock market? Between 1986 and 2012 there were 7 negative years out of 27. In approximately 1 in 4 years the UK stock market was losing money; in 3 out of 4 years it was gaining. This shows why the general trend is upwards with stock market investments.

If we look at rolling 5 year periods only 1 in 7 periods were negative over the same data period, even through the dramatic falls due to the credit crunch. Does this surprise you? This shows that the longer you invest your money, the lower the likelihood of you losing money. This cannot be guaranteed, but it shows how the market works in practice.

If we examine the same data with 10 year rolling periods there were no negative periods. Therefore, over an even longer period you are even less likely to lose money.

This shows overwhelming evidence that you should consider investing your money for longer-term goals such as retirement funds.

## Don't put all your eggs in one basket

The best way to manage risks is to diversify your portfolio. This can be achieved by increasing the number of holdings. If you hold 1 company share in your portfolio and this fails, then you lose 100% of your investment. If you hold 50 companies equally, and 1 fails, you only lose 2%.

You can extend this concept to different types of asset (split between cash, fixed interest, shares and property), different geographical locations, and currencies. In theory, the wider you diversify the smoother your returns. Research shows that this approach limits the downside of your portfolio without too much impact on the upside.

It is impossible to pick which asset class will be the best or worst performing in any given year. The solution is to prepare a split of assets so that you are best prepared to take advantage of good years with certain assets, and smooth out poor years with others.

## Asset allocation

Portfolio construction starts with asset allocation. This is the choice of which assets to use, and in what proportion. This will be put together with a medium to long term view, and have a combination of assets that will work together to deliver the risks and returns you want. Various academic research papers have analysed investment portfolios and have concluded that the majority of a portfolio's performance over time can be attributed to this part of the process.

If you have come to the conclusion that your current asset allocation needs some work then start thinking about how you can make this stronger. This is the most difficult part of the process for non-professional investors.

## Timing your entry into the investment market

When is the best time to invest money? Most people instinctively answer that it is when the market is at the bottom. When is the best time to sell out of investments? Most people tend to answer that this is when the market is at the top. This sounds easy and logical doesn't it? The reality and the practice are very different, and this is one of the reasons that amateur investors consistently lose money compared to professional investors.

The reality is that it is not possible to predict when the right or best time is to invest your money. The only real option is to invest for the medium to long term.

It can be tempting to try to make short term gains on portfolios by moving in and out of different markets. Even with very strong market and economic data, this is almost impossible to get right every time.

You should not try to guess the market, since even fund managers get this wrong, with far more detailed data than you possess. Research shows that if you miss the best few days in a market rally you can lose almost all of the returns. For most people it is not possible to react that quickly. For this reason, portfolios should be put together on the basis of delivering longer term performance rather than taking active short term bets.

## Market turbulence

In turbulent stock market periods it can be tempting to reduce the risk of your portfolio by biasing the portfolio more towards safer assets. If you do this, all you do is to hamper future performance in the longer term, or even lock in losses. Trust in the process of the portfolio and markets, so that you can benefit from any recovery in the market. A big stock market fall in one period is usually followed by a big gain afterwards. These periods of turbulence are less important over time.

If you are particularly worried about stock market volatility you could consider staging in your investment buys. This will have the effect of averaging out the volatility in the market.

## Take account of inflation

Inflation has an underestimated impact on returns over time. Often people focus on the actual rates of return without reflecting on the impact of the increase in the cost of living.

Inflation is currently lower than historical averages, but cash savings are still currently losing money in real terms. Bank accounts will grow in actual terms, but will lose money in real terms to inflation. In contrast stock markets tend to perform ahead of inflation over time. Over even longer periods the differences can be staggering.

## Reviewing your progress

You should review the progress of your investments towards your long-term goals. Over time, your goals will change too. Build in a regular review to ensure that you are up to date with your investments and that they are on track to meet your goals.

## Rebalancing your portfolio

Naturally, each of the assets contained in your portfolio will perform in a different manner. Over time, better performing assets will form a larger proportion of your portfolio, and therefore alter the risk of your portfolio. To minimise the risks of this happening, at future reviews you should switch funds back towards the ideal asset allocation.

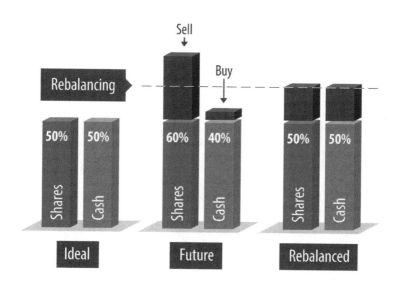

Imagine that your ideal portfolio split was split 50% between cash and shares. This is unlikely to be the case, but it neatly explains the concept. Over time, you would expect that the shares would grow faster than the cash, but that both should grow in value. So in the future you might expect that the shares become 60% of your portfolio and cash 40% (of a larger pot). In this case you would be taking greater risk than you previously wanted. Therefore you should rebalance your portfolio back to the 50/50 split you previously set. This is how you can control the risks you take in your portfolio.

Without taking action like this you run the risk of dramatically increasing the risks you take in your portfolio. I have regularly seen the effects of this with long-term portfolios which have never been reviewed. The result can be that people who would prefer lower risk end up holding high-risk portfolios.

## Types of liabilities

Your liabilities are the opposite of your assets. It makes sense for you to understand more about how these work.

### *Mortgages*

It is very common to hold a mortgage on a property. This is a loan which is secured against the value of your property. This means if you do not make the contracted payments you may have the property repossessed. The fact that the property can be repossessed means that the risk is lower for the lender. Since they have some security for their capital, the interest rates tend to be lower than with other forms of credit.

The cost of buying a property tends to be high, so we typically borrow over 25 years or more. Despite having relatively low interest rates it is not uncommon to repay 2-3 times the value of the property in interest over the term of your loan.

In recent years there has been a property boom, which has inflated the value of properties in the UK. This has given us 2 problems. The first is that the cost of buying a property has dramatically increased. This means that many first time buyers have been effectively priced out of the property market. The second issue is that many people wrongly think that the increase in the value of their property makes them richer. Your main residence is not a true asset in Financial Planning terms since if you sell it you need to have somewhere to live, and need to buy another property. Many people have ignored this issue and have continued to borrow against their increased "equity" in the property – the difference between the market value of the property and the amount they owe. While this is a relatively low-cost form of borrowing, this is effectively mortgaging your future self, especially when you borrow to repay shorter-term debts or to fund your lifestyle.

Another issue is that many people have interest only mortgages. This means that you do not repay the capital on this loan. If you do not put a plan in place to repay this capital at the end of the mortgage you run the risk of losing your home.

You should aim to repay your mortgage as soon as possible.

### Loans

Personal loans are a short-term form of credit and are typically unsecured. This means that they tend to be much more expensive than mortgages although they will be more flexible. In general terms you should aim to clear your personal loans as soon as you can.

### Credit cards

Credit cards are the most flexible forms of credit, but also the most expensive. It is not uncommon to see credit cards charging 30% interest. While these cards provide you with convenience, they also represent risks that you will overspend on your lifestyle expenses. You should control your credit card use.

### Other

We often use credit but do not necessarily view it that way. For example, you may purchase car or home insurance but elect to pay monthly. Often this comes with a credit agreement, which increases the cost of the overall policy. You may also use other forms of credit such as interest-free credit when you buy a household item like a sofa. You should be aware of the effect that these credit arrangements have on your expenditure. These convenient sources of credit may help you to budget for items like car insurance, but they do mean that you can end up buying things you may not have otherwise been able to afford.

## Good liabilities vs bad liabilities

Just like there are good and bad assets, there are also 'good' liabilities and bad liabilities. I use 'good' with caution in the case of liabilities since

I generally believe that the sooner you can become debt free the sooner you can become financially independent. In general, our society has become hooked on credit. We see this in all parts of society, from the Government, to business to individuals.

## Bad liabilities

Most liabilities are bad. They sit in your bank's asset column, and are there to increase the bank's profits. Bad liabilities take away income from your future self, and hold back your ability to accumulate assets, which in turn holds back your ability to get to financial independence. You should look to reduce and remove your bad liabilities as soon as you possibly can.

Bad liabilities include the following:

- Mortgages
- Personal loans
- Credit cards
- Payday lending
- Interest-free credit

## Good liabilities

Some liabilities can be considered to be 'good' so long as you are prepared to accept the additional risks that these liabilities bring to you. In general terms, a 'good' liability is one that someone else pays on your behalf. An example of this would be a buy to let mortgage. If your rental income is £500 per month, but the mortgage is £400, then essentially the tenant is paying for your debt. Eventually, your tenants will purchase the property for you. From this perspective, the debt is 'good' since it is not holding back your asset growth; in fact, it can be helping you to grow your assets.

While this is true in many cases, it does come with additional risk, so you should enter into such arrangements with caution. Ultimately, your tenant does not own the liability – you do. Therefore, if something goes wrong, or the market changes then you can be left with a very expensive debt, and you alone will be liable for that debt. While property prices and rents are increasing, this should not be a problem. But if you buy at the wrong time you can find that this debt can work quite dramatically against you. If you multiply the debt by taking multiple properties, then you can quickly find yourself in financial trouble.

## Gearing

Borrowing can increase the levels of return that you make on investments, but it can also accelerate losses too. This is why borrowing to invest should only be taken if you are an experienced investor and you understand the risks you are taking. Unfortunately, many people invest in property based on the 'advice' of estate agents, who have no liability for this assistance, and are merely seeking to establish a sale.

Let's look at an example of gearing:

Let's say you borrow £75,000 to buy a property worth £100,000. The cost to you is £25,000. If the value of that property goes up by 10% your asset is now worth £110,000. Your equity in the property is now £35,000. This growth in your equity is now a return on your investment of £25,000 of 40%! But what happens if the reverse takes place? What if the asset loses 10% value, and is now worth £90,000? In this case your £25,000 investment would now be worth £15,000, and you would have lost 40% of your stake.

| | Initial purchase | House value increases by 10% | House value drops by 10% |
|---|---|---|---|
| Value | £100,000 | £110,000 | £90,000 |
| Loan | £75,000 | £75,000 | £75,000 |
| Your stake | £25,000 | £35,000 | £15,000 |
| Change in your stake | n/a | £10,000 | -£10,000 |
| Percentage change in your stake | n/a | 40% increase | 40% decrease |

You can see that the borrowing has amplified the growth or loss in both cases. It acts to increase the volatility of your investment.

# Becoming debt free

Becoming debt free should be one of the key aims of your financial plan. When you become debt free you will be well on the way towards financial independence. This is because you will be living within your means, and using your excess income to provide for your future.

## A real sign of financial maturity

Becoming debt free is a real sign of financial maturity. It shows that you can manage your budget and all of your financial efforts will go towards building your assets, rather than someone else's assets. You will go from mortgaging your future to building your future.

## Not merely paying on time

Paying your debts on time is <u>not</u> a sign of financial maturity. Your bank might reward you by giving you access to more credit, but this is just to keep you on the hook. Paying your debts on time merely prolongs your servitude to banks and credit, and holds back the day when you can be truly working towards your future.

## 0% deals

Moving your credit card debt to different providers is a clever move. It allows you to stop paying the interest on your expensive credit card debt in the short term. Remember that these introductory deals always revert back to a much higher interest rate after a period of months.

While this move makes sense if you have significant credit card debt, just remember that this is not a sign of financial maturity either. The temptation may be to allow yourself to reduce your outgoings for a while and spend the savings. This can only lead to more overspending if you do not sort out your debt issues. You need to combine the interest savings with reductions in the capital you owe.

## Paying off debts early

You should build a plan of action to get yourself debt free as soon as possible. This will be hard work initially, but will reap rewards for your future self in the longer term.

## Plan of action

If you are in debt your first course of action is to first face up to the problem, and then focus on clearing the debts as quickly as you can. You should do this in order from the most to least expensive by interest rate. Let's illustrate this with an example.

John has a mortgage, a car loan and 2 credit cards. The debts stack up like this:

| Debt | Amount owed | Interest rate | Term remaining | Monthly payment | Total interest |
|------|-------------|---------------|----------------|-----------------|----------------|
| Mortgage | £100,000 | 4% | 20 years | £606 | £32,569 |
| Car loan | £10,000 | 9% | 4 years | £250 | £1,933 |
| Credit card 1 | £7,000 | 20% | 5 years, 7 months | £175 | £4,631 |
| Credit card 2 | £3,000 | 28% | 9 years, 10 months | £75 | £5,805 |
| Total | £120,000 | | | £1,106 | £44,938 |

In the above examples, I have assumed that the credit cards require a minimum monthly payment of 2.5% of the balance. The term remaining for the credit cards assumes that you do not add to the balance, which is unlikely!

Where would you start in the above example?

Start with the highest interest payment first, and then continue down the list in order of interest rate. This should yield you the best return on any over-payments.

Dan Woodruff

Let's assume John has an additional £100 per month available.

If he takes this additional money and overpays on the most expensive interest rate he would choose credit card 2. He would increase his monthly payments to £175 per month. This would have the following effect:

Just on this credit card debt, he would make the following savings:

- The debt would be paid off in 1 year and 11 months, knocking an incredible 7 years and 11 months off the term
- This would save him £4,929 in interest!

John could then take his £175 per month and apply this to the remaining balance on credit card 1. Assuming he had made the same minimum payments then after 1 year and 11 months his debt would be £5,465. He would have 3 years and 9 months remaining.

If John now pays £350 per month towards this debt, the following would happen:

Just on this second credit card debt, he would make the following savings:

- The debt would be paid off in 1 year and 7 months, knocking an incredible 2 years and 2 months off the term
- This would save him £1,398 in interest!

John would now be 3 years and 6 months into this plan. Remember, he has only committed an additional £100 per month towards his debt reduction plan, but he has already cleared £10,000 of debt and saved £6,327 in interest.

He would now have 6 months remaining on his car loan, with a balance remaining of £1,398. John could now apply his additional £350 per month saved to paying additional capital off this loan. This assumes that the loan terms permit overpayments.

Just on this loan debt, he would make the following savings:

- The debt would be paid off in 3 months, knocking 3 months off the term
- This would save him £17 in interest.

Overall, after 3 years and 9 months John would have cleared £20,000 in debt and saved £6,344 in interest.

But let's not stop there. Now, let's assume John continues paying the money saved towards his mortgage.

By now his mortgage balance is £86,785. John has 16 years and 3 months remaining. If he overpays by £600 per month, he would make the following savings:

- The debt would be paid off in 6 years and 11 months, knocking 9 years and 4 months off the remaining term
- This would save him £13,473 in interest.

By the end of the process John would have repaid all of his £120,000 debt after 10 years and 2 months – that's in almost half the time. This is just by overpaying by £100 per month! Could you find £100 per month to save a total of nearly 10 years and £19,817 in interest? Imagine what £200 per month could do!

If you want to start looking at your own debt situation, check out our debt calculator. See **7figuresplan.com/resources**.

## Figure 5 – Total useable assets

Figure 5 in your action plan is your total useable assets. This means your total assets less your 'bad' assets. Figure 5 would exclude your main residence (this is a liability). It would also exclude cash accounts such as your emergency fund and your other allocations for short-term expenses such as tax, holidays or projects. It is important to exclude these non-useful assets since they can cloud your vision as to where you are in your planning, and make you feel more prosperous than you actually are.

Figure 5 will include assets like the following:

- Investment property
- Pensions
- Savings and investments
- Business assets
- Other saleable assets not linked to short-term spending

What you are left with is the amount of assets you can use towards your future financial independence. This is an extremely important figure.

## Figure 6 – Total liabilities

Figure 6 in your action plan is your total liabilities. This should be fairly easy to calculate as it is the sum total of all your debts. Don't forget to include those sneaky interest free credit items:

- Mortgages
- Personal loans
- Credit cards
- Other
    - Loans from family
    - Interest free credit

## Using figures 5 & 6

Both Figures 5 & 6 are extremely important to the 7 Figures Plan since they are the driving force behind your future financial independence. You should use them together to calculate your net worth, but should not focus on this figure too much. Figure 5 is much more important to you than your total assets minus your total liabilities.

Figure 5 is the key to your future financial independence. If you manage to build Figure 5 to a level where you can fund your future Figure 4 (your expenses) then you will manage to become financially independent.

## Figures 5 & 6 on the timeline

Let's examine how we can visualise these figures on your timeline.

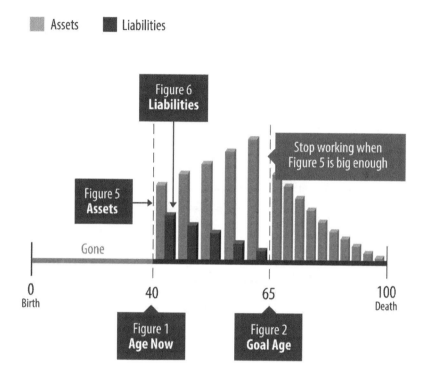

As you can see, you have an amount for Figure 5 on your timeline, plus an amount for Figure 6. It is possible that when you do the exercises at the end of this chapter you might be surprised to discover that you have less in useable assets than you had thought. Don't beat yourself up about this; instead use the concepts in this book to motivate you to build more useable assets. Focus on reducing and wiping out your Figure 6, so that you become debt free. The sooner you can do both of these tasks, the sooner you can build Figure 5 to allow your future self to become financially free.

## Chapter summary

- Assets drive forward your future financial independence and liabilities hold this back
- Understand how compound interest works – get started as soon as you can
- Understand how different types of assets work well for various needs
- Work out how much emergency fund you need, but strike the balance between not enough and too much cash
- Consider complex investment decisions, or outsource this area
- Understand your liabilities are the bank's assets
- Some liabilities can be 'good' if someone else is paying for them, but remember that borrowing to invest creates additional risk
- Becoming debt free should be a core goal
- Track the growth in your assets and plan to reduce your liabilities
- When you have enough assets to fund your expenses you will be financially free

## Action plan

- Use the workbook at **7figuresplan.com/workbook**
- Complete assets vs liabilities template
- Work out your ideal emergency fund
- Consider which of your assets are good assets v bad assets
- Prepare a debt action plan and examine our debt calculator

# Chapter 7 - Figure 7 – Protection

Figure 7 is an area which sits slightly apart from the other figures in the 7 Figures Plan. However, this area can have a profound impact on your family's security.

## Disaster planning

This chapter is designed to get you to think about all the disasters that could happen to your family. This will help you to clarify which you should focus on, and how to minimise the impact on you if the worst was to happen.

Most of these scenarios are very unlikely to happen, but you should not let that lull you into believing that they cannot happen to you. You should prepare for the worst so that if this does happen you are not affected more than you need to be. We all know stories of disaster in families we know. In many cases the financial implications are as bad as the other issues. We cannot stop disasters from happening, but we can minimise their financial impact.

### Disasters happen when you least expect them

Some time ago I took on a new client, let's call him Jim. He had just received an inheritance from his uncle, and wanted advice on how to best use these assets to prepare for his future. This is a typical scenario for us, and we got to work.

When we prepared his Financial Plan it became clear that there were issues with the ownership of a property, which was nominally his, but was actually jointly owned. He had previously been married, but had never resolved the ownership of a joint property bought during the marriage, since the mortgage company would not release his former wife from the debt. After they split up, his former wife moved out and Jim lived in the same house for many years, continuing to pay the mortgage.

Jim sensibly used the proceeds of his inheritance to pay off the remaining mortgage of his home. Effectively, this meant that his former wife increased her assets since she was still joint owner of the house. This property issue was serious enough for me to recommend that he consult a solicitor before paying off the mortgage.

In fact he started this process but died suddenly a couple of months after our initial meeting. He had been ill in the past, but clearly was not expecting to die so suddenly. He died without resolving property ownership issue, but after he had paid off the mortgage. His will stated that his 2 children should inherit the property, but jointly held properties usually pass directly to the survivor, outside of your will. This led to complications for his children after his death, who had to fight their mother for ownership of the property. As you can imagine, this was not an ideal family situation!

What this shows is that when disasters strike, they happen quite suddenly. Had Jim realised he was about to die he would have taken action on the property sooner. Not many of us know the date of our death, so we are better served by preparing as if it is just around the corner. Sometimes, as in Jim's case, it just might be.

### My story

At the beginning of this book I shared my story, and in particular how a serious illness to my mother changed not only her life but also our financial security.

When my mum was diagnosed with multiple sclerosis she was still able to get around and do most of the things she had always done. She was a busy mother, had a job and did what she needed to do to provide for her family.

Gradually her condition took hold and eventually she had to stop working because she could not manage to do the regular committed hours that most employers wanted. This meant that she had to rely on State benefits to provide for her family. If you have been in this position you know that this means subsistence living at best. Life became hard for her in many ways. She had to deal with the physical and emotional aspects of a serious medical condition. While this happened, her financial situation was getting worse. She had her house repossessed, and this left her with a mortgage debt that was impossible to repay on the income she was left with.

Why do I tell this story? When these disasters happen we rightly focus on the illness that the person is going through. We don't talk about the money. But can you imagine a different story, where my mother had instead an insurance policy to fall back on? With more money coming into the household maybe she would not have had to move away from her friends, and maybe she could have had a little more financial security while she was dealing with all the physical changes of her illness.

## Risks

Which risks should you be concerned about in your personal situation? It depends on your family position and your view on the risks involved, as well as your budget. Here are some major risks to think about.

### Death

The death of a bread winner is an obvious risk. Whether this is a concern for you depends on whether you have a partner and a family. If you are single, this is unlikely to be a significant concern to you. If you have a family, you will probably want to be sure that their lifestyle is not reduced if you or your partner is not around to provide for them.

Think about what would happen to your family if you or your partner were not around to provide and care for them. Apart from the obvious emotional impact, there would be the loss of an income to take into consideration. Then there could be additional issues around child care with one less person to look after children. The long term effects could be significant.

If you own a business, the risks could be significant. In the absence of formal agreements, sole traderships and partnerships will be wound up on death. This can cause complications for your family. Limited company shares will be passed in your will, and could cause issues for those left behind, especially if they have no interest in running a company.

### Illness

Serious illness is another significant risk. This is a much greater risk as medical advances mean our life expectancy grows. You are much more likely to get sick for an extended period during your working lifetime than you are to die. Despite this, more people take out life insurance than sickness insurance. This is partly because sickness insurance costs more. Why does sickness insurance cost more than life insurance? It is because sickness is more likely to lead to a claim than death.

Think about what would happen to your lifestyle if you or your partner were too ill to work. You would still retain most of your current expenditure but your income might suffer. The longer the illness lasted the worse your financial position would get. The long term effects could be far reaching.

### Loss of income

If you are unable to work for other reasons such as redundancy this could put you and your family in much the same position as sickness. Without an income your financial position would quickly worsen, with significant long term effects.

# Possible solutions

There are various steps you can take to minimise the financial impact of serious disasters on your family. You can use insurance, or more practical measures.

## *Death*

### Emergency fund

If an adult in the family dies the survivor would be very glad to have some readily accessible cash. On your death some of your assets could be tied up in legal paperwork, and it would be easier for the survivors to have ready access to cash to fund their lifestyle and other expenses like your funeral.

### Insurance

The obvious solution to the death of an adult is to take out insurance. This is often done to cover a mortgage. While this is sensible, this does not answer all the needs your family would have if someone dies.

You can take out various forms of life insurance. Most policies are term assurance. These policies are relatively cheap and would pay out a lump sum if someone dies. Often this would be used to repay the mortgage debt.

Consider what other needs your family might have if you or your partner dies. For example, it might be good to have security in your home with the mortgage repaid. Once this is done, how will the surviving partner or children pay their bills with the loss of an income to the family? They will still have to pay the usual household expenses (think Figure 4) even with one less adult in the household.

You can take out additional insurance to cover these expenses. This can be in the form of a lump sum or as a replacement income. This is known as family income benefit.

Life insurance is relatively cheap assuming you have no pre-existing medical conditions.

Your employers may offer death in service benefits. Often this is expressed as a multiple of your salary (1 to 4 times your salary). This should come to your dependents tax free, and can supplement your other provisions. Just remember that this would be lost if you changed job.

If you set up life insurance you should consider using a trust. Trusts are a legal structure to hold assets outside of individual ownership. In the case of life insurance, if you die and a claim is made on the policy, the proceeds can pass to a trust instead of directly to your family. From the trust, the family avoids inheritance tax on the money and also gets their hands on the money quicker. This is a complex area so you should seek legal and financial advice before setting anything up.

Will

A will is a legal document, which allows you to deal with how your assets are treated after you die. It allows you to set out your wishes on other important matters. Your will allows you to stipulate who gets what when you die. You can also use a will to avoid tax on your death.

Despite this it is estimated by the BBC than only 3 in 10 adults in the UK have a will.

You know that it is inevitable that you are going to die one day. A will allows you to decide how your assets will be treated after you die, as well as other important matters. This can include:

- Who you want to receive your assets when you die?
- How will your dependant children be looked after?
- Who is going to manage the paperwork when you die?
- What happens if those you want to benefit die before you?

When someone dies it is obviously a distressing period for their family.

Having a will can help to make this time more straightforward than it might be otherwise. Often bereaved relatives find it difficult to make decisions. By having your affairs in order, you can take away a part of the stress of this period.

If you die without making a will, the law decides who gets your assets. This is called intestacy, or dying intestate. The law will determine how your assets are distributed after you die. This is unlikely to work how you would have planned. In some cases, intestacy can spell disaster for your family. If you are married, your spouse will get some of your assets, but not necessarily all of your assets. Any children would get some of your assets. If you are not married, your partner gets nothing. If you have step-children they would not get anything.

Dying without a will means unnecessary complications. You should expect that your assets will not be distributed in the way you would have chosen.

The benefits of making a will:

- Control
  If you make a will, you get to decide where the money goes after you die. This is important in terms of control, but it can also give you peace of mind that your loved ones will be provided for. You can make specific provisions for certain people, and ensure that money eventually ends up with the right people.

- Tax efficiency
  A key benefit to making a will is the ability to avoid inheritance tax. Wills are a great way to put your tax affairs in order so you can ultimately shelter assets from inheritance tax.

- Practical issues
  Your will enables your affairs to be put in order so your family

does not have to do this after you are gone. Your will should ensure that the money ends up with your family more quickly.

## Business agreements

If you run a business you should consider what would happen to that business if you die. This depends on the legal structure of the business. If you run a company, it is likely that you own some or all of the shares in the business. In the event of your death these would pass to your spouse or family under your will (if you have one). Would your spouse or family want to control a company? Would they have the inclination or ability to step into this role? What would your business partners think of this arrangement?

If you run a partnership, and you do not have a formal agreement in place, the business will be wound up on the death of a partner.

There are many agreements that can be put into place for this type of scenario. This is especially important when you have more than one director or shareholder. Often businesses set up life insurance alongside an agreement that allows either the business or the surviving family of a deceased director to exercise an option to force the sale of the deceased's shares. The life insurance proceeds can then be used to purchase the shares. This leaves the company to continue under the management of the remaining directors, while the deceased director's family get cash for the shares. This is a complicated area and you should seek legal and financial advice before taking action.

## Discussing death

I know that you do not want to consider your death, and that it is a difficult area to discuss. Take some time to think about what would happen when you die. Would your family be ready to put into action your plans? Would they know about all of your solutions like the life insurance, wills and other arrangements. It makes sense to put together some instructions so that this is clear when you die.

## *Sickness*

### Emergency fund

This is the situation where you would be most glad to have a fund of easily accessible cash. If you are too ill to work it is likely that your income will reduce quite quickly. If you are ill for a relatively short period of time you will be glad of a pot of money to tide you over and to maintain your standard of living while you are recovering. You should put aside funds to cover *at least* 3-6 months worth of expenses.

### Sick pay

If you are employed your employer will probably offer some sort of sick pay arrangements. You should look at your contract of employment to understand your entitlement. Don't make assumptions - many people misunderstand their sick pay entitlement. They often believe that their employer would be far more generous than their contract of employment actually states. Knowledge is important here, so you can plug any gaps if necessary. It is common for employer sick pay to be paid for a certain period of time. After that you will move on to statutory sick pay or state benefits. These are likely to be much lower than your salary. In some companies you may be entitled to receive income protection insurance once your sick pay ceases.

### Insurance

Insurance can be used to plug any gaps you have left after you become too ill to work. This tends to be through critical illness insurance or income protection insurance. Critical illness pays a lump sum (or annual income) if you are diagnosed with a serious, named illness of a specified severity. There are a number of serious illnesses covered by these policies, and most companies have signed up to minimum standards in this area. The plan would pay out if you were to be diagnosed with a serious illness that was likely to kill you within a year or so.

Income protection works by paying you an income if you are too ill to work. This usually has a wider definition of illnesses as it is not the illness that is important but whether you are too ill to work. Thus, income protection tends to pay out in more cases, and would include stress-related illness and back problems, which would not be covered by critical illness.

Some employers offer one or both of these covers, so it is important to check how much cover you are entitled to get.

If you do the figures and see that you have a gap between your current income and what you need in the event you get ill, you can take out insurance at your own cost. I would recommend that you consider this.

Lasting power of Attorney

A Lasting Power of Attorney is a very important document, and one which most people overlook unless they get advice from a professional. This document allows you to appoint a trusted person such as your spouse to act on your behalf in the event that you are incapacitated due to illness or accident. You can override this at any time, provided you have the mental capacity to do so.

You can appoint your Attorney to act on your behalf in relation to your health and welfare, and/or your property and financial affairs.

You can only set up a Lasting Power of Attorney while you have the mental capacity to make decisions. If you become mentally unable to take decisions, the Courts will appoint a Deputy to work on your behalf. A Deputy works very much like an Attorney, but has the added problem of strict Court oversight.

There are 2 types of Lasting Power of Attorney. You can use either type or both.

- Health and welfare Lasting Power of Attorney
  This type of Lasting Power of Attorney is used to allow you to make decisions in advance about how you will be treated in

certain circumstances related to your health. You could use this to decide whether you access nursing care, or whether you want to receive certain medical treatments. This type of Lasting Power of Attorney can only come into action when you are no longer capable of making decisions on your own.

- <u>Property and financial affairs Lasting Power of Attorney</u>
  This type of Lasting Power of Attorney is used to allow someone to control your financial affairs. Usually, this is used to allow a trusted person to control your assets such as your property or investments; however, it can be as simple as allowing someone to pay your bills on your behalf. This type of Lasting Power of Attorney can come into action at any time, whether or not you have the mental capacity to make decisions on your own.

The process for setting up a Lasting Power of Attorney is a bit more involved than it used to be. You now need to complete the relevant forms and register the Lasting Power of Attorney with the Office of the Public Guardian. You can do this yourself, although it is usually advisable to get legal advice since this document can mean that someone will be taking important decisions on your behalf. These issues should be understood fully before making such a commitment.

You can cancel a Lasting Power of Attorney at any time, provided that you still have the mental capacity to make decisions on your own. You cancel your arrangements by issuing a 'deed of revocation' which is a straightforward letter revoking your previous instructions. This must be registered with the Office of the Public Guardian. Lasting Powers of Attorney cease automatically following certain events such as divorce.

<u>Michael & Anne's story – what can happen without a Lasting Power of Attorney</u>

Michael and Anne are a married couple in their early 60s. Michael was a City executive while Anne had taken time out of work to bring up their

4 children, and was now working in a part-time role. They came to us when Michael suffered a serious brain injury after an accident, which immediately affected his mental capacity. Unfortunately, the couple had never considered that such an accident could happen, and had never set up a Lasting Power of Attorney. After Michael's accident it was too late to put something in place because Michael did not have the mental capacity to sign the forms.

Their house was jointly owned, but because Michael had a higher paying job he built up more value in his retirement plans. He also had an insurance policy which paid out a large lump sum after the accident.

Unfortunately, Michael's medical situation meant he had to go into a nursing home quite suddenly, and much sooner than they had expected. In the absence of a Lasting Power of Attorney, Anne was appointed as his Deputy. This is the legal process that exists for people without the required documents. While this process is quite similar in many ways to how a Lasting Power of Attorney works, the Court took a harsher view as to how Anne should manage their assets than Michael and Anne would have done if they had been free to act on their own. The Court decided that all of Michael's assets should be used to fund his nursing care. The practical implications were that Anne was suddenly without funds, and could not access Michael's pension funds or insurance pay-out. Since nearly all of their useful assets were in Michael's name Anne was suddenly left without any capital or income. Of course, if Michael was able to voice his opinion he would never have sanctioned such a move.

Happily, the situation was partly resolved but only after months of costly legal action. Eventually, after a year Anne was allowed to use some of Michael's income to fund her lifestyle, but only under some strict controls. If they had set up a Lasting Power of Attorney they would have avoided all these problems and Anne would have been able to run their finances as she chose.

Think about your own situation. What would happen to your loved ones and assets if the Courts step in and take control of your finances? If your loved ones would not be taken care of, you should consider making a Lasting Power of Attorney.

Everyone should set up a Lasting Power of Attorney, just as we should all set up a will. The process is relatively straightforward and means that your wishes will be followed if you are unable to make decisions on your own. This should be done now, while you are fit and able to, not left to when you get too ill to make a difference.

Redundancy

If you are employed you can cover some of your expenses using redundancy cover. This would pay you a monthly income if you are made redundant but usually this would only continue for up to 12 months. The idea of the cover is that it gives you a buffer to pay your important bills while you secure a new job. The cover is quite limited in that it usually will only allow you to cover bills related to a mortgage. The self-employed cannot qualify for this cover since you control whether you work or not.

## Current needs versus future needs

This is an advanced part of protection, but is very important. It is relatively easy to work out what your current needs are. If you are unable to work due to illness you can work out what your short-term expenditure needs are and provide insurance cover to give you an income to pay these bills.

This approach works for the short-term, but what about the longer-term? How do you take into account the future needs of you and your family? In the case of replacing income this is usually done by providing increasing cover. The cover would rise in value each year to take into account increases in the cost of living. This does not take into account possible increases in living standards as your income goes up, so you need to keep your cover under review.

What about death? I often see people who have set up cover to pay off their debts and mortgage in the event of death. This is a good place to start. But this ignores other equally important issues for the future prosperity of your family. Think about it. What would happen if you died tomorrow? Let's assume that your spouse has the mortgage paid off. That would reduce their expenditure and provide a level of security. However, they would still need to maintain that property and pay many or most of the expenses that they have now; all this would apply without your income and practical support. With only 1 adult there may be increases in costs such as child care. Obviously this depends on your situation. Thinking about the future needs of your family might mean that you take out far more cover than you would have previously imagined. This could be used to provide for their future income needs, perhaps until the children are educated.

## Figure 7 on your timeline

How do you use the elements of this chapter to ensure that you and your family is secure no matter what happens?

Relate the cover you have got back to your timeline. You can examine the ongoing income versus the expected expenditure in the event of an illness. This will quickly show you whether you have enough cover in place to provide for you. The same can apply to your family in the event of early death. You can examine the ongoing expenditure for those who remain, and work out the income or lump sum you would need.

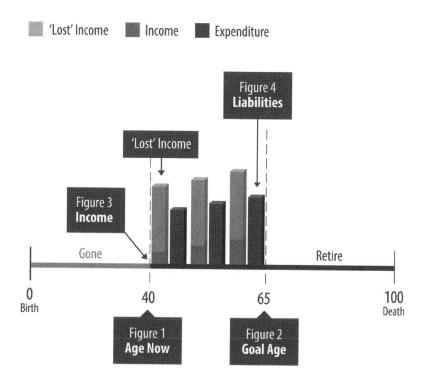

In this example, you can quickly see that the theoretical death in the family reveals a 'lost income', which means that the family would have less income than expenditure. If they try to carry on paying the same expenses as before they would quickly eat into their cash reserves and eventually run out of money. This could happen relatively quickly without suitable cover in place.

## Chapter summary

- Disaster planning is about protecting what you already have
- Think about the risks of death, illness and loss of income in your family, and the effects this would have on your income and expenditure, assets and liabilities
- Various products exist to insure these situations
- Practical documents are also important, such as wills, power of attorney, trusts and business agreements

## Action plan

- Use the workbook at **7figuresplan.com/workbook**
- Calculate what you would need in the event of illness, death or redundancy
- Calculate what cover you have in place
- Work out what cover you would need to protect what you have got
- Consider cover to protect future needs as well
- Consider setting up wills, Power of Attorney, trusts and business agreements
- Discuss arrangements for family and leave instructions

# Chapter 8 - The 7 figures plan

Now you have examined all the important areas of your plan and calculated the 7 figures you will need, we can bring this all together in a way that can help you to make sense of it all. This will help you to take some intentional action.

## Bringing together all the concepts

This chapter brings together all the concepts highlighted in this book. We will show you how the different key figures act together.

### Visualise your future

You must understand where you want to go. Paint your picture so this can motivate you and keep you focused. This may be quite difficult for you but will give your plans some direction and momentum.

### Decide your strategy

The 7 Figures Plan cuts through all the noise and focuses on only the important figures. Of course there will be exceptions to this, but this strategy will allow you to get the maximum results with the least distraction. Experience will guide you to avoid costly mistakes.

### Simple so you can take action

The 7 Figures Plan is simple on purpose so that you can **take action**. It is not knowledge that will get you to a secure future. It is not desire that will get you to a life of your dreams. It is not even a plan that will get you there. Only by taking action will you get the results that you want for your financial future. The sooner you start then the sooner you will begin to see results. Yes, you may make mistakes, but you can use these to learn and correct your actions towards a better future.

## Easy to understand where you are now

By stripping back all the various layers of your financial life you can see where you are now with your money. This simplification helps you to gain a real understanding of what is important. I want you to understand where the action must be taken to get the maximum results, hopefully in the shortest period of time. Time is your most precious resource and it is running out. Therefore you had better start taking action as soon as possible to make the most of your future resources.

## Can see progress – motivational

This focus on 7 Figures allows you to see progress with the action you take. This will take time, but in the future when you look back on the work you are doing now you should be able to see perceptible movement in the right direction in all of the indicators that I have given to you.

The result should be motivational for you. I know it is for me. When I look back on my past goals I can tick them off. I realise just how far I have come. Sometimes it can be frustrating while you are putting in the hard work. This is especially true in the beginning of a long-term project like your future financial security. However, the hard work needs to be done early to get the project moving. Think of it like this: the energy needed to move a heavy object like a ship is enormous at first. The initial speed is slow, but once it gets moving the energy required to keep it moving at that speed is less.

I want the 7 Figures Plan to motivate you as early as possible so that you do not give up before you start to see movement in the key figures. Therefore I expect you to be able to use the simplicity of the figures I have presented to you to be able to allow you to see real progress.

### Keep coming back to it

When you revisit your 7 Figures Plan you will be able to see the progress that you have made. This will be relatively small at first, but over time you will amaze yourself with the acceleration in the results you are making.

You will also be able to correct your course as things do not go quite as planned. This will help you to avoid any nasty shocks in your planning later on. You should also get motivation as you see results.

## Priorities – suggested order for action

Everyone is different when it comes to planning their financial needs. However, in general I suggest that you work on taking action in the order set out below. This will give you the best chance of getting the right results in the shortest period of time. Naturally, you might identify one of the later issues is more important to you. In some cases you should apply these principles in a different order, or work on some at the same time. If that is the case then move the issue up your priority list. Just remember that experience has taught me that this is the right order to follow. Do not ignore the other issues just to focus on one. Believe me when I tell you that I have seen more people than I can remember who have not heeded this advice and have later regretted it.

### Priority 1 - Spend less than you earn

Unless you get control over your budget you will never be able to become financially secure. This applies whatever you earn. The first priority should be to spend less than you earn. Only then can you put the excess income after expenditure towards your future priorities. This applies to you whether you earn an average wage or are a high earner. I have seen many examples of high earners who spend more than they earn and build up massive debts.

### Priority 2 - Emergency fund

Most people I meet do not have a large enough emergency fund. It is difficult to build the right amount of free cash but it is very worthwhile. I have seen countless examples of people who have had to take drastic action to shore up short-term issues by mortgaging their future in some way. If you have the right amount of cash free to use whenever an emergency strikes you will have much more security. You will also avoid the typical trap of using debt to pay for short-term expenditure. In the long term this will save you massive amounts in interest, and you will get to your goals faster. You will also avoid the trap of dipping into your longer-term savings, and therefore avoid holding back your future goals.

### Priority 3 - Protect what you have got

This is all about disaster planning. Insurance costs money, but the cost is relatively low when compared to what may happen to your finances if something dramatic happens to you. Think about the major issues that could strike you and your family: death, illness, redundancy, flood, fire etc. Spending in this area should be targeted but will help to keep your finances secure no matter what happens. Personally, I feel much happier knowing that if the worst happens my basic standard of living will be covered.

### Priority 4 - Pay off debt

Becoming debt free should be a key ambition if you want to be truly financially secure. Remember that your debts are someone else's assets. Your budget is not under control if you are borrowing to pay for current lifestyle expenses. If you have built up debt in the past then do not worry. You can become debt free in a relatively short period of time. After that, all of your resources can go towards building your secure future, not someone else's.

### Priority 5 - Save for the future

Although this is the last of the priorities it is actually the most important. The paradox of these priorities is that the others are more urgent, since their impact can be more immediate. Put another way, if you do not follow the priority order I have suggested then you could find your whole plan in trouble if something unexpected hits you.

However, without getting to the issue of saving for your future, you will not have a secure future. Therefore, do not put this priority off for too long as this will set back your plans.

Saving and investing will allow you to build up the assets you need to become financially independent. In the long run this will give you the resources you need to be able to choose not to work. That must be your ultimate goal, because if you get to that point then you have achieved financial security. You will then start to have the ability to make your own future.

# Conclusions from the 7 figures plan

You now need to do some work to gather all the figures needed for your 7 Figures Plan, if you have not already done so. This will allow you to make an analysis of where the weaknesses are in your finances. After that, you can decide what action needs to be taken.

## *Identifying weaknesses in your plan*

Time between your age now and your goal

Take a look at your age now (Figure 1) versus your goal age (Figure 2) on the timeline. This gives you a visual perspective on the work that must be done to get to where you want to. If the gap between these ages is relatively small then you are either going to have to work particularly hard, take much more risk, or you are going to have to adjust your expectations. Your goals must be realistic. If you have a goal to retire in just a few years then you are going to need either the assets or the income to be able to justify this.

Spending vs earnings

Examine the relationship between your income (Figure 3) and your expenditure (Figure 4). This is a key determinant of your future prosperity and security.

## Underspending

The way you look at this relationship depends on your outlook. If you are cautious in your assumptions or are restricted in your ability to earn, then you may want to focus more on your expenditure (Figure 4). If you can bring your spending down, you can allocate more resources towards your future.

## Overearning

If, like me, you believe that you have the ability to earn more, then you can focus on increasing your earnings to exceed your spending. This distinction could be the subject of another book entirely, but it is vital to how you tackle the relationship between income and expenditure. Either you will focus on reducing your lifestyle expenditure now for the sake of your future by keeping your spending under control or you will try to grow your income to become greater than your spending. The latter is more fun, but comes with some peril if you are not skilled at growing your income or are not honest with yourself about your spending.

It can be tempting to say that you will grow your income later and save towards your future later. But later might not come. You can only secure your future by taking action now. Do not delude yourself into thinking that you can solve your issues by just earning more money. You need to work hard at generating greater income, and you also need to keep an eye on your expenses so that these do not rise in line with your income.

Keeping your spending under control is also important, but not at the expense of living a full life now. Remember the story of my mum. She got ill at age 35 and died when she was 50. Live your life now, but just remember that you might also live to 100!

*Overspending*

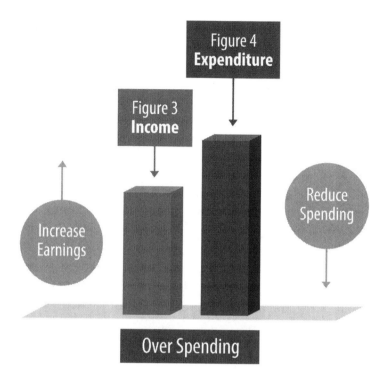

Overspending occurs when you spend more than you earn on a regular basis, If this is the case then it is likely that you are building up debt to pay for your short term expenses. This is the road to disaster and must stop. Only by getting control over your spending will you be able to plan for the future. Stop thinking that things will change one day and take action now.

*Solution 1 – reduce spending*
You need to go back to your budget and seriously examine all of your spending. Look at the list and mark down everything that is essential. This includes items like your debt repayments, tax, food and other household expenses. Then look at what is discretionary. There will be certain items that you can cut out straight away, to bring your expenses back below what you are bringing in. You do not necessarily need to cut

out items altogether. You can negotiate with suppliers to reduce your expenses. For example, it is relatively easy to reduce your mobile phone tariff, or get your entertainment supplier to reduce their bill to keep you as a customer.

*Solution 2 – increase earnings*
The other alternative is to bring in more money. It is not fun to cut back on your spending, and most people do not naturally do this. The only other realistic solution is to find other ways to bring in more money. This might mean taking a second job, or selling items to bring in some extra income. You could look at getting a pay rise from your employer. If you do not curb your spending then you will need to increase your income. Just remember that increasing your earnings often increases your spending. If nothing else, you will pay more tax when you earn more money. You need to factor this in and earn even more to counter this problem.

If you are not prepared to take one of these steps then put this book down as I cannot do anything to help you.

*Subsistence*

Subsistence occurs when you spend what you earn on a regular basis. This is the default position for most people. This is a better position than overspending, but only slightly. By spending what you earn you leave your finances open to problems in the future. It is likely that you are not saving enough for the future and you probably do not have enough put aside for emergencies.

Go back to the principles of the previous section and re-examine the spending patterns. Your choices are the same. You either need to reduce your spending or to increase your income. Your goal should be to generate more excess income that can be put towards your longer term priorities.

*Surplus*

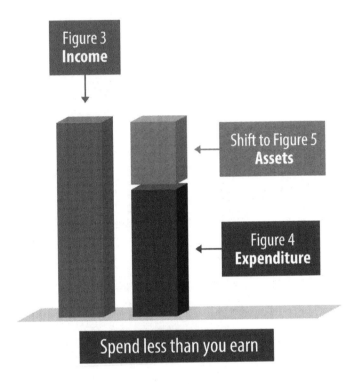

You have a surplus if you spend less than you earn. Obviously, this is the ideal position. The amount by which you can underspend or overearn is directly linked to the amount you can put towards your future. The more that you can underspend or overearn the faster you will get to your goals.

*How much should you put towards your future goals?*
The amount that you put towards your goals will shape your future. You should put the maximum available towards your future goals, but of course this has to be shaped by your short-term priorities and your available resources.

*Priorities, goals and resources*
The exercises at the end of Chapter 4 will help you to put together a list

of your goals and priorities for these goals. Review these goals in the light of the available resources you have. You can examine the relationship between your income and expenditure (Figures 3 & 4), and start to put this available money to good use.

*Short term put what you can save to good use*
Your short-term goals are easier to identify and plan for, since they are probably smaller and more easily obtainable. You will need to work out the money needed to achieve these goals and to put aside a budget to go towards reaching these goals.

*Your ultimate number*
Longer-term goals will be more difficult to plan for. You should start with the end in mind and work backwards from there. Your first task should be to work out how much is enough – your ultimate number. You will need to put together all of your goals, attitudes and assumptions and do some calculations regarding the amount needed for your goal. You can then start on a plan to build up the assets necessary to put you in the position to achieve your goals.

This is probably the most difficult aspect of your plan to get right. Your assumptions and calculations could easily go wrong if you make the wrong decisions. For example, you might miss out a vital aspect in your assumptions such as the changes caused by inflation. Take some time over this area, and be cautious in your assumptions. You are better off by far if you err on the side of caution than if you make bold but unobtainable assumptions. Revisit the sections on this subject in chapter 4.

You should end up with a number to aim for. Once you reach this number you should be in a position to achieve your long-term goals. Despite this, you will need to review this number as your circumstances and goals change over time. The problem with Financial Planning is that you change so much over your lifetime! Events will change your perspective and move you in different directions. Remember that the whole purpose of your 7 Figures Plan is to get you to take action, and as soon as possible.

This number is likely to be much larger than you would expect. You may be shocked when you realise just how much you need to secure your future. This very much depends on your goals, your circumstances, your age and your expectations.

*Your ultimate number – how much should you save?*
Once you know your ultimate number, you can then work backwards to examine how much you need to put aside to achieve this figure. This could give you a monthly figure that you could save towards this goal. Do not be put off if this seems like an impossible figure at the moment as there are always ways that you can address the problem, so long as you work at it and are realistic. Remember that you need to chip away at the goal gradually and over time.

Assets vs liabilities

Examine the relationship between your assets (Figure 5) and your liabilities (Figure 6). The difference between the 2 figures is the basis on which you can build a secure financial future for yourself and your family. If you have done your homework from the previous section, you will have a number written down, which will represent your long-term goal. You will know that if you reach this figure, your financial security will be guaranteed.

At the start of your planning this will be the weakest area. You will know your ultimate number and attaining it will seem a long way off. The purpose of the 7 Figures Plan is to motivate you to take action and to continue taking action. This is what will get you results in the end. Remember, we will help you to get rich slowly.

The gap between your ultimate number and the difference between Figures 5 & 6 represents the weakness in your assets. Ultimately, this will show you how much is left to do to reach your goal of financial security.

*Measuring progress*

If you do anything as a result of this plan, it should be in this area. Once you have gone to all the trouble of measuring the relationships between the other key figures, your key focus should be on this area of your plan. I believe that when you get to the point that you can easily measure the difference between Assets and Liabilities (Figures 5 & 6), then this will be the key driver of your future progress. As you start to see your action and behaviour towards money start to make a difference to these figures, then you will build up your motivation to make further and faster progress.

*Reducing liabilities*

We covered this area extensively in earlier chapters, but you can obviously make a plan to reduce your liabilities as a key method of increasing the difference between Figures 5 & 6.

If your liabilities are greater than your assets then you are currently in a particularly weak position. The higher your liabilities are, then the greater the work you must do to solve your financial issues.

If you get your liabilities down to zero then you will have more money to put towards increasing your assets. You will also stop paying interest to other people and institutions. Ultimately, this will speed up your progress towards financial security. Make a plan to reduce your liabilities to zero.

*Increasing assets*

Eventually you must increase your assets to reach the figure you have identified as your ultimate number.

If your assets are low now then this will represent a weakness in your financial plan. The lower your assets, the farther away you will be from reaching your ultimate figure.

You can build on the strategies you have learned in this book to put your savings habit to good use. You will probably need to invest in some sort of financial product, or find your own method for growing your assets. Some people invest in property; others build a business; most people invest their savings in financial products.

You can do this yourself if you are prepared to make mistakes as part of your learning. The alternative is to employ an adviser to help you in this area. The downside is that you must pay for this advice.

Ultimately, you must decide whether you have the time and inclination to learn the skills to be able to manage your growing assets. The advice route should be more secure for you in the longer-term if you do not want to be hands-on, and also want to avoid making costly mistakes along the way. Neither is right or wrong; you just need to decide which is best for you.

<u>Emergency fund</u>

This is a key short-term goal in your financial planning. If you do not have an emergency fund or this is not of the correct size, then you seriously risk your Financial Planning unravelling if some sort of financial disaster comes your way. Believe me, this will happen to you, and has probably happened to you in the past. If you do not address this weakness in your planning then at some point this will hold back your progress towards your ultimate goals in the long-term.

Work out the figures you need for your emergency fund using the principles in Chapter 6. Once you know this figure, you can compare your instant access savings to the result. If you do not have enough then this must become a short-term goal as you have a weakness in your plan to resolve. If you have too much, this represents an asset you can use towards other short-term goals. Alternatively, you can take any excess not needed for emergency planning and short-term goals and instead put this towards longer-term goals. Do not fall into the trap of holding too much cash.

Remember, your emergency fund should not overlap with other short-term funds like your money for tax, your holiday fund or any other short-term goals. Your emergency fund should be separate from other short-term funds and should not be part of your longer-term projects. Be honest with yourself in this area.

<u>Protection</u>

This area is a weakness for many people. You can easily overlook the potential risks of ill health, death and redundancy. After all, they probably will not happen, and you may prefer not to consider them. You can also underestimate the cover you will need in each area. Your attitudes and budget will determine how much you decide to put towards this area, but do not make the mistake of underestimating the size of the potential issues.

Protection is almost always an area where we can help clients to make improvements. Most people tend to cover the basics like their mortgage debts. They usually forget to insure their cost of living and ignore the fact that their family's lifestyle needs are often greater than the costs of their mortgage. Of course security for your family's housing is important, but do not lull yourself into a false sense of security in this area if you have your mortgage covered. The chances are that you need to do more.

Identify the gaps in your family's financial needs if certain disasters happen, and to either put aside money to cover these, or more likely to set up insurance policies to pay a lump sum or income should those events come to pass. The peace of mind this will give you will be worth the cost. If the worst does happen you will be extremely glad of the time and effort you have put into this aspect of your planning.

## *Where can you make improvements*

You need to understand the key weaknesses in your Financial Planning so that you can take action in these areas. Fundamentally, most weak Financial Plans suffer from one or more of the following issues:

1. <u>Spending too much</u>

2. <u>Not earning enough</u>

3. <u>Not saving enough or at all</u>

4. <u>Not protected enough or at all</u>

5. <u>Relying on debt</u>

If you can solve all of these habits you will have the blueprint for future financial security. It's simple isn't it!

## *How to improve your situation*

<u>Work longer</u>

Think back to Figure 2 – your goal age. If you examine the difference between your Ultimate Figure and your current assets and resources, then you might come to the conclusion that you are never going to reach that Ultimate Figure within the timeframe you have allowed. This means that your expectations are unrealistic and your timeframe is too short. One solution could be to revise Figure 2 and to put back your goal age. The longer you have to save the more your assets could grow. Also, if you need to rely on your resources for a shorter period in later life, then you need to build up less money to fund your financial independence.

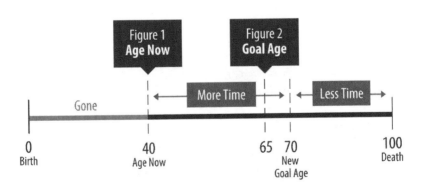

Of course, the reality of this situation is that it will mean you spend more time working, and less time doing what you really want to do.

Adjust future expectations

Instead of working longer, you might instead decide to reduce your future expectations. This is the most likely event to happen if you do not take concerted action now. If you do nothing and carry on as you are, you could end up sleepwalking into a future where you *have* to reduce your expectations if you decide not to keep on working. Remember, a decision to take no action now is actually a decision to lower your future expectations. This does not sound like much fun to me, but is a potential solution. You may decide that you might be prepared to accept a lower standard of living in later life in exchange for not making an effort to plan for this future now.

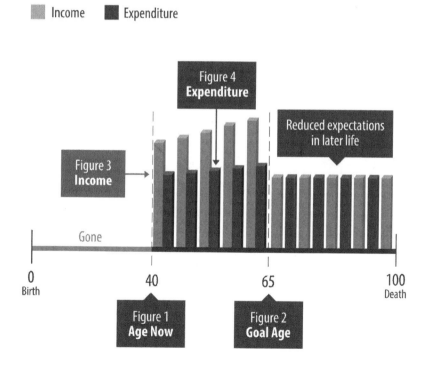

Earn more

I firmly believe that we all have the capacity to earn more. This is obviously one way out of the problem of not having enough money to save, or if you identify that the difference between your Ultimate Figure and your current resources is just too great. Instead of putting back your goal age (Figure 2) you could instead decide to earn more now. This seems like a more palatable solution to me. I would much prefer to work harder now to reap the rewards at a later date than to need to work longer later because I missed the boat.

Solutions here could be to secure a pay rise, to take a second job, to start a business on the side, or to learn new skills to increase your earning potential. This area is probably outside the scope of this book, but I know from personal experience that the more hard work I put into the development of my own skills, then the greater my earning potential has become. This in turn has led me to being able to put more towards my long-term security. The road is long and full of plenty of hard work, but with careful application and smart decisions you can start to leverage your skills in ways you might never have imagined.

Spend less

The alternative to earning more is to spend less now so that you can spend more later. Personally, I dislike this notion and my experience tells me that most other people do too. It can be difficult to rein in your spending. To be honest, it is not fun! You do have a responsibility to balance your spending in the present so that you do not rule out prosperity in your future. Whatever you do, never use debt to fund lifestyle expenses now. I do not advocate some sort of harsh and boring existence now in exchange for a rosy future later. Besides, there is a limit to which you can rein in your spending. You still need to buy food, heating and other necessities of life.

Nevertheless, spending less is an option and can be combined with earning more to great effect so that you can release money towards your long-term goals.

<u>Take more risk</u>

Another solution could be to take greater risks with your assets now. This works on the principle that in general the greater risk you take with your money, the greater returns you should expect, on average over time. Remember that there are no guarantees in this area. However, sensible risk management of your investments should yield dividends in the long-term. If your analysis shows that you need more assets to achieve your goals, then a good solution could be to take greater risks with the aim of growing assets faster. If this works out then the amount you need to save from income should be less than if you take smaller risks. This solution will not be for everyone, but should be considered because it can have a massive effect over the long-term.

<u>Take smarter decisions</u>

There is not one perfect solution to your Financial Planning – if there was then this book would have been much shorter. Of course, there are many gurus out there who peddle silly theories about how you can use one simple method to get results. The reality is that you need to put all of these methods to use to chip away at the edges of your overall goal.

If you earn more, spend less, adjust unrealistic expectations, plus take sensible and calculated risks then you will be making your money work harder for you in the long-term. Address all the obvious weaknesses I have identified and you will build your future finances on a firm foundation.

This takes hard work and dedication but it is the only way for you to build the skills necessary for future financial security.

## Putting it all together

The 7 Figures Plan is designed to simplify things. If you can focus on just a few key financial numbers then you will be able to easily measure your progress. By measuring your progress you will be able to see the results of your action. This will motivate you to take more action and to correct the mistakes you make along the way.

To download your own copy go to **7figuresplan.com/workbook**.

The 7 Figures Plan fits onto one page on purpose. This gives you a simple snapshot of where your finances sit now, and how far away you are from your Ultimate Figure. You will discover where you should focus your attention most so that you can put your resources to work to make improvements.

By keeping this focus simple, I want to encourage you to take action. By reducing your focus to key areas, you will be able to put aside all the complexities of your finances and to zero in on what really needs your attention.

By measuring your progress over months and years you will be able to see where you have come and how far you have to go to reach your goals.

## Reviewing the plan

So you have worked though all the exercises in this book, and have come up with a financial action plan. Well, unfortunately your work is not done. You are not going to put your plan together only to stick it in a drawer. If you do that, you will soon run out of steam and will soon forget all about your plan. You will drift back into your old habits and you will lose direction.

Remember, you are building your financial muscles. If you want to keep progressing, you need to keep building your skills and growing your habits.

Therefore you must review your plan regularly. How often you perform this review is up to you.

### Why review?

The 7 Figures Plan is designed to keep you focussed on the important, key figures in your life. A review will help you to correct your course and to see the progress you are making. Remember that journey from London to Edinburgh? You might hit a diversion from time to time, but you can also use your 7 Figures Plan as a kind of dashboard to measure progress from London, and towards Edinburgh. You will use the 7 Figures Plan to measure your financial progress away from your current situation and towards your secure financial future.

How to review

There are many ways you can review your progress. The 7 Figures Plan is designed for you to take a simple snapshot of your financial position so you can easily extract the top level data you need to make informed decisions about your financial progress.

The 7 Figures Plan is a process. This discipline means you will not miss anything out. Without forcing yourself through this process you run the risk of consciously or unconsciously ignoring inconvenient truths. If you do this you may focus only on the things that are going well or that you like to do.

You could also try asking yourself some straightforward questions such as:

- What has gone well in the last period?
- What could I have done better?

The point of these questions is not to chastise yourself if something did not quite go to plan. This will always happen so you had better get used to it. Aim to identify those habits that lead to good results so that you can replicate these again in the future.

By asking yourself about the things that did not go quite to plan you are not trying to pass blame or self-recriminate. Focus on how you can avoid these habits in the future. Realise that mistakes will occur. Your reviews should help you to avoid making these mistakes more than once. By reviewing your errors you might identify what went wrong, and then take the action to stop this happening again.

Let's look at an example. Imagine that your goal is to pay off your credit card debt. You have a card charging a high interest rate and have a large balance on it.

At a 3-monthly review you use the 7 Figures Plan to take a look at your balance and work out that it has actually increased in that period. You could beat yourself up about this as you will know that it will be your fault that you did not manage to generate extra disposable income to pay off some of the capital. Or you could blame your boss, spouse, kids, the economy or whatever else your creative brain comes up with.

Instead, if you take a look at your actions over that period and ask yourself what you did correctly, and what could have gone better you will get two results from this.

The first is that you can focus on some positive actions that you took, no matter how small. For example, you might tell yourself that your credit card balance grew only slightly despite a whole variety of factors against you. Be careful not to fall into the trap of making excuses though. That will do you no favours for the future. You might say to yourself that although you did not pay off some of the balance, at least you have identified that there is a problem early enough to do something about it. You need to work on building your financial confidence. The alternative is paralysis and inaction.

The second consequence of the review is that you can aim to analyse where and why things went wrong. This will lead you to some important conclusions where you can take some positive actions to turn the situation around. So, going back to our example, you might identify that you overspent on your discretionary spending. This might prove to you that you do not plan your monthly spending well. Perhaps you bought too many lunches when you could have made your own lunch. There is likely to be a pattern if you take the time to look for it. The more you train yourself to look, the better you will become at resolving these issues. The solution could come in many forms. You might say to yourself that you need to cut back on your unnecessary spending. This is a bit boring and will only get you so far. Or you might say that you need to plan your spending better. Or you might decide that you are going to approach your boss and ask for some extra projects or work that could lead to additional income for you. All of these ideas are potential solutions. You just need to train your mind to take the necessary strategic steps and stop avoiding taking action.

## Regularly

The most important thing is to monitor your financial progress regularly. Use this to measure how your assets change. Updating your 7 Figures Plan should not be difficult or consume much time once you have started. The fact that it is simple and on one page means that you can use each version to compare to the previous one. How often you undertake this review is up to you, but I guarantee that if you apply the principles in this book then you will start to see progress. When you look back over where you have come from over time you may be surprised by just how far and how fast you have come. I do this myself from time to time in my business and financial plans, and am always surprised by just how far I have come. The same will be true for you if you just keep working gradually on the principles I have set out for you.

## Monthly

I like to measure progress monthly. The changes are small, but it keeps me focussed on where my spending habits are taking me. I measure my budget monthly just to keep track of short-term issues like overspending.

## Quarterly

It can be difficult to focus too far into the future, so it is useful to have a quick review every 3 months. You can set yourself small goals to reach as kind of staging posts for your long-term goals. Those long-term goals probably seem far off and perhaps unobtainable. By taking concerted action to chip away at these goals you will start to accelerate your progress. Addressing your 7 Figures Plan quarterly might help you to see small progress towards short-term goals, and how you are changing the relationship between your assets and liabilities.

3 months is long enough to get things done, but not too long into the future to correct your course if things haven't quite gone to plan.

## Yearly

Quite a lot can change in your life in a year, but the years can pass quickly if you do not take the time to undertake a regular review.

I recommend that you reassess your long term goals fully at this point. You will find that your outlook changes as your family situation develops and you get more into planning your financial future.

## When big changes happen

If something major takes place in your life you will need to review, no matter whether this fits into your schedule or not. This might be a major life event such as marriage or the birth of a child. It might be something unexpected such as serious illness or unemployment. Alternatively, it could be the results of your hard work, such as a promotion at work or the achievement of one of your goals.

Aim to constantly drive your progress forward. When you get good results you should build on this as this will motivate you to achieve bigger and better things. Do not allow yourself to sit back when you achieve small goals as you could fall back into unproductive habits.

## Small steps lead to big results in the end

What is the point of all these reviews? In the end it is all about you taking consistent, directed action. If you take action on a regular basis this will definitely add up to results. The results might not take the course that you had originally planned, but this might work in your favour. The only thing I can definitely predict is that if you take no action you will get no results.

By forcing yourself to take these regular small steps, you will get to your larger goals in the end – one step at a time. If you regularly review what went well and what could have gone better you will find that you get faster at achieving your goals since you continue to take action only on the things that work.

## Conclusion

Regular reviews are so vital that there are many books written on the subject. You will never become an expert at reviewing but you will get better if you try to stick to certain principles. All successful people review in some way. This might be through a formal process, by using an adviser or mentor, or via some other method. The review process helps you to understand what you do well. Reviews build your confidence to do more of the same. Reviews also help you to analyse where you go wrong, and take action to stop this happening again.

## Chapter summary

- Bring together the 7 figures to give your finances some strategic direction
- Visualise your future so you can set a strategy
- Simplify what is important to aid understanding so you can take action and see progress
- For most people your priorities should be to:
    - Spend less than you earn and use the excess towards your future
    - Establish the right level of emergency funds
    - Protect what you already have
    - Pay off any (bad) debts
    - Save towards your future
- Use the 7 Figures Plan to identify weaknesses in your current arrangements and make improvements
- Review your plan regularly so you can see trends, progress and correct problems

## Action plan

- Complete the 7 Figures Plan in your workbook
- Complete the action planner to start your plan

# Chapter 9 - Hiring a financial planner – what to look for

You might think that this is a strange subject to address at the end of this book. The fact is that some of you will get to this point and will be honest enough to admit that you need help. Remember that I have simplified many of the complex topics in this book to get to the heart of the issues. Why? So I can encourage you to take action towards your future.

## Why might you want to hire a Financial Planner?

To me, there are 2 main reasons:

### I need technical help with a specific problem

You may decide to plan your financial future yourself. I applaud this since this means you are taking the action to build the skills necessary to build a better life for yourself and your family.

However, experience has taught me that at a certain point we are better off not spending the time to learn a certain skill when we could hire in an expert to do things faster, better and more efficiently.

As an example, what would you do if you wanted to build a wall in your garden?

You could just look up a few videos on Youtube on brick laying. How hard can it be? Armed with some bricks and mortar plus a few tools, you could launch into your project. You would get a result of sorts, but would it be the wall you pictured in your mind? I doubt it. You would also spend money acquiring tools. You might have to concede defeat and look to an expert to undo all your mistakes and start again. The result might be lost money in materials and tools, and extra costs in undoing your mistakes, plus time delays.

You could go on a night course in brick building over 6 months to learn the skills necessary to build a basic wall. You might find that you have the natural aptitude for this process. There would be an inevitable delay in starting your project and you would still need to buy tools and materials. The result should be better under this method, but it would definitely be slower.

The alternative might be to pay an expert who has learned all the mistakes there are to learn and all the shortcuts and professional methods. The result would be a professional job done in the minimum of time. The only downside would be that you would have to pay for this result. I would argue that unless you intend on building walls on a regular basis it is uneconomic to try to develop the skills in this area. The time and money you spend on developing skills here could be better spent on earning money to pay for the builder, or acquiring other skills that you could leverage in the future.

If we apply this example to Financial Planning there are many scenarios where you might want to consult an expert who can quickly and efficiently guide you through the process. Usually this comes down to wanting to avoid costly mistakes with your money, especially when the decisions made cannot be reversed.

Usually new clients consult with us due to some sort of pain in their financial lives. This can be any of the following significant life events

- Retirement decisions
  Can I afford to stop work, and will I run out of money?
- Divorce
  How will a loss of assets affect my future?

- Inheritance
  How can I use an unexpected windfall to secure my future?
- Bereavement
  How will my finances change now that I have lost my partner?
- Serious illness
  What does this mean for my future security?
- Buying a home
  How does this change my finances?
- Tax planning
  What is the most efficient way to manage my complex affairs?
- Managing investments
  How can I maximise my capital growth or income within the
  risks I want to take, in a complex market?
- Selling a business
  How much do I need to sell the business for to secure my
  future?

If you follow the 7 Figures Plan you will inevitably come to a point where your knowledge will need the help of a trained and experienced expert. It is not a weakness to employ a professional to solve the problem you have identified. In fact, it makes complete sense.

## I want this problem off my desk

You might seek professional financial advice for a related but different reason. You either do not have the time or the inclination to do the Financial Planning yourself. Our clients have the ability to learn about Financial Planning. Of course they do. In fact we go out of our way to educate them in the reasons for taking the right decisions in their finances. However, most of our clients are either busy with their career, family or business and want to devote their time to these pursuits since that is the whole driving force for them wanting a better future.

If time is an issue for you then you need to be realistic about this. If this is the case then it makes sense for you to hire in an expert in Financial Planning to guide you through the process quickly and efficiently. Sure there will be a cost, but this will be a price worth paying to avoid the costly mistakes you may have made in the past when you did not follow through on your actions or listened to those you shouldn't have.

You may not be the type of person who wants or enjoys analysing your financial position. You are obviously interested in this area but you know that you are better off spending time making money, enjoying time with your family, or other lifestyle pursuits. Again, there is nothing wrong with this. After all, what is the point of Financial Planning if it is not to release you from the burdens of hard work? You should focus on building a secure future for yourself and then enjoying your lifestyle. If hiring in a Financial Planner is the right move for you then I fully support you.

## 11 clever questions to ask a Financial Planner which give you an unfair advantage

Let's assume you have made the decision to hire a Financial Planner as you either have a technical issue to deal with or you do not have the time or inclination to undertake the work yourself.

Your next problem is to find a Financial Planner who you can trust to deliver the right result for you. There are good advisers and bad advisers. There are very few who are completely untrustworthy, thankfully, due to tight regulation. Despite this, it doesn't necessarily follow that all advisers will be the right fit for you.

We have prepared some clever questions for you to use when interviewing a potential adviser. These are designed to help you identify the untrustworthy, inexperienced or unqualified.

### Question 1 - What are your qualifications and experience?
Ask your financial adviser how long they have been working with clients *like you*, since the answer may surprise you! Be specific, because many advisers tend to be generalists, and may not have the right level of expertise to deal with your situation. Qualifications are important, but are not everything. You should be able to make a judgement based on

their all-round knowledge and experience.

Do your research on qualifications since some people have impressive sounding titles, but often these are meaningless.

## Question 2 - Explain your Financial Planning process

Many financial advisers do not really have a defined process for how they work. This means that their services can be patchy since different advisers within the firm work in a different way. It is important for a properly run business to have a defined service standard and process, so that others within the business can pick up your case where relevant or necessary.

Your financial adviser firm should have a clearly articulated process for all forms of client communication and research. This should be relevant to your personal needs and situation.

## Question 3 - What are your services and how are they relevant to me?

Ask what services are on offer. Many firms do not have a clearly identified service package, which can make it difficult for you to decide which is right for you. We segregate our services by typical client needs, and we do not service all types of client. Of course, your needs may not fit neatly into a package, but a service standard is a good place to start so that you know exactly what you are buying. We often find that clients come to us when they have experienced a problem with a previous adviser, perhaps because the expected levels of service were not defined at the outset.

## Question 4 - How do you conduct research?

It should go without saying that your financial adviser should be well-positioned to offer you research which you would find difficult to perform yourself. As an example, we run the following research systems which enable us to effectively research our clients' needs. Don't assume that your adviser has access to all these tools, because they might not!

- Financial Planning software
  This allows us to accurately project a client's lifestyle now and into the future, and enables us to help them to make decisions based on facts. In our experience, few firms are willing to help you in this vital area.

- Investment software
  We run an amazingly complex investment analysis tool which allows us to compare and research the many thousands of different investment products and funds out there. Too many firms we come across provide investment analysis based on the free tools given to them by insurance companies. If the tool comes from the provider, how independent will their recommendations be?

- Product research
  We run 3 separate systems to compare the features of products (since they are not all the same), the costs of products, and also the mortgage market. Many adviser firms only focus on the costs of the products they recommend, which is only part of the story.

- Comprehensive systems
  Many adviser firms have hundreds or even thousands of clients. How else can they keep tabs on their clients various complex needs without the aid of a comprehensive system. The one we use enables us to cope with different client types, all their financial products and situations. We can do instant investment calculations for them, and more importantly set up a series of tasks so that we never forget to perform services we have signed up to do.

Question 5 - What values drive your business?
This may be overlooked, but it should be important for you to think about how well the values of the business fit with your own. Failure to do this can result in frustration and a breakdown in the relationship.

## Question 6 - Have you ever had any complaints or regulatory breaches?

Has the financial adviser or firm ever been subject to a complaint or regulatory or ethical breach? This can be checked via the FCA Register (see the resources section). If they have, you may wish to question whether the same might happen to you. Incidentally, our firm has never been subject to any of these issues.

## Question 7 - Where do you specialise?

If you require specialist help, such as financial planning or investment management, you will need the help of a specialist adviser. Very few advisers can be a true specialist in everything, so ask them what they work on the most.

## Question 8 - What is your status with the regulator?

All financial advisers should be regulated by the FCA (but some aren't so you should always check). Be very wary of anyone giving financial advice who is not regulated because this can mean you could lose out heavily if something later goes wrong. We have seen many instances of unregulated advisers freely giving out investment advice in areas that they have little experience. Their clients run the risk of serious losses with no back up from the system if something goes wrong.

## Question 9 - Are you restricted in the advice you give?

Is your adviser independent? Many firms look like they are independent but work using a panel of products which benefits the adviser or their firm in some way. There is nothing wrong with being restricted in the advice they give as there could be many good reasons for this. The important thing from your perspective is for you understand the reasons why the adviser's self-imposed restrictions will be of benefit to you.

## Question 10 - How is your adviser paid?

Ask your adviser how they are paid on an ongoing basis. Few people realise that their adviser often gets some payment on an ongoing basis without them realising it. If the adviser gets an ongoing payment from you, you should expect an ongoing service! We are very clear up-front with our clients on this matter.

<u>Question 11 - Can you see client testimonials and case studies?</u>
Finally, ask if you can see client case studies on how they have helped people in the past in a similar situation to your own. Also, a decent financial adviser should be able to give you the names of some satisfied customers, who would be happy for you to speak to them to explain how they have been of benefit.

## Chapter summary

- Even if you manage your own financial affairs there may be many times when you require some expert financial assistance
- Most people approach a financial planner when they are anticipating or experiencing a major financial life change
- Others use a financial planner since they need technical help or they just don't have the time to do the work themselves

## Action plan

- Use our questions to interview your candidates if you decide you want to work with a Financial Planner

# ABOUT THE AUTHOR

Dan Woodruff is a Financial Planner who works with people who are anticipating or navigating significant life-changing events. He helps them to focus on what's important in their lives so that they can take action now to use their money to live their best possible future.

Made in the USA
Charleston, SC
15 July 2016